The Administration of the Sacraments to Dying Non-Catholics

A DISSERTATION

Submitted to the Faculty of the School of Canon Law of the Catholic University of America in Partial Fulfillment of the Requirements for the Degree of

DOCTOR OF CANON LAW

BY THE

REV. JAMES IGNATIUS KING, J.C.L.,

OF THE ARCHDIOCESE OF ST. PAUL.

1924.

Nihil Obstat.

THOMAS J. SHAHAN, S.T.D.,

Censor Deputatus.

Washingtonensi, Die XXVII Maii, 1924.

Imprimatur.

MICHAEL J. CURLEY, D.D.,

Archiepiscopus Baltimorensis.

Washingtonensi, Die XXVII Maii, 1924.

TABLE OF CONTENTS.

PREFACE

The investigation of problems connected with the administration of the Sacraments is always of interest to a priest. At the time of approaching death, such ministrations become particularly useful and important. But at this moment precisely, when Providence and circumstances provide so many factors which speculation is unable to control, their discussion is most difficult. The purpose of the present study, then, has been practical rather than speculative, namely, to explain the canons in the Code which concern the administration of the Sacraments to dying non-Catholics.

The term non-Catholic, as used in the subsequent pages, is perhaps employed in a somewhat arbitrary fashion. Our Lord Himself defined its limits in the words, "He that heareth you, heareth Me, and he that despiseth you, despiseth Me." In short, all those who do not accept the teaching of the Church, either through ignorance or for any other reason, are considered as falling within the scope of the present dissertation.

The problems which arise in connection with ministrations in the dying moments of such persons, as the writer realizes full well, are hardly capable of complete analysis in a treatment which is primarily canonical. Difficulties arise on every side, but the effort of the writer has been to honestly present what are his findings and convictions. If they are not altogether satisfactory, a novice can hardly be criticized too severely, where even the greatest theologians dispute.

BIBLIOGRAPHY.

(The method of citation used is indicated in brackets after the work in question, if any abbreviated form has been employed.)

Codex Iuris Canonici Pii X Pontificis Maximi jussu digestus Benedicti Papae XV auctoritate promulgatus, Romae 1918.

Acta Apostolicae Sedis, (AAS), Romae 1909-.

Acta Sanctae Sedis, (ASS), Romae 1865-1908.

ALPHONSUS, ST., *Theologia Moralis,* Torino 1887.

Ante-Nicene Fathers, (ANF), *The,* 10 vols. (American Reprint of Edinburgh Edition), New York 1899.

AUGUSTINE, P. CHAS., *A Commentary on the New Code of Canon Law,* vol. IV, V, Third edition revised, St. Louis 1923.

AYRINHAC, H. A., *Marriage Legislation in the New Code of Canon Law,* New York 1918.

BELLARMIN, CARD. ROBERT, *Opera Omnia,* Neapoli 1872.

BENEDICTI XIV, *Opera Omnia,* Tom. XVI, Prati 1846.

BILLOT, *De Ecclesiae Sacramentis,* Ed. V, Romae 1915.

BILLUART, CAROLUS, *Summa Sancti Thomae, Ed. nova,* Parisiis.

BLAT, ALBERTUS, *Commentarium Textus Codicis Juris Canonici, Lib.* III, *Pars* 1, Romae 1920, *Lib.* III, *Partes* 2-6, Romae 1923.

BUCCERONI, IANUARIUS, *Casus Conscientiae,* 2 vols, *Ed.* V, Romae 1903.

BONAVENTURA, ST., *Opera Omnia, Tom.* IV, Quaracchi 1889.

Canones et Decreta Concilii Tridentini, XIX reimpressio stereotypa, Taurini 1913.

CAPPELLO, FELIX M., *De Censuris,* Augustae Taurinorum 1919.

CAPPELLO, FELIX M., *Tractatus canonico-moralis de Sacramentis,* I, (Augustae Taurinorum 1921), III, (Augustae Taurinorum 1923).

Catholic Encyclopedia, 15 vol., New York 1907-1912.

CAVALLERA, FERDINANDUS, *Thesaurus Doctrinae Catholicae,* (Thesaurus), Parisiis 1920.

CHELODI, IOANNES, *Jus Poenale,* Tridenti 1920.

Collectanea Sacrae Congregationis de Propaganda Fide, (Coll.), 2 vol., Romae 1907.

Corpus Juris Canonici, editio Lipsiensis secunda post Aemilii Ludouici Richteri curas ad librorum manu scriptorum et editionis Romanae fidem recognouit et adnotatione critica instruxit Aemilius Friedberg, 2 vol., Lipsiae 1922.

Corpus Scriptorum Ecclesiasticorum Latinorum, (CSEL), *Cypriani Opera*, Vindobonae 1871.

D'ANNIBALE, CARD. JOSEPHUS, *Summula Theologiae Moralis, Ed.* III, Romae 1892.

DE SMET, ALOYSIUS, *De Sponsalibus et Matrimonio, Ed.* III, Brugis 1920.

DE LA TAILLE, MAURITIUS, *Mysterium Fidei*, Parisiis 1921.

DENZINGER-BANNWART, *Enchiridion Symbolorum et Definitionum*, (Denz.), *Editio decima quarta et quinta quam paravit Ionnes Bapt. Umberg*, Friburgi Brisgoviae 1922.

Dictionnaire Apologetique de la Foi Catholique, Tom. I (Paris 1907), II (Paris 1911), III (Paris 1916).

FERRERES, P. IONNES, *Compendium Theologiae Moralis*, 2 vol., *Editio undecima, quarta post Codicem*, Barcinone 1921.

FRANZELIN, CARD., *Tractatus de Divina Traditione et Scriptura, Editio tertia*, Romae 1882.

GASPARRI, CARD. PETRUS, *Tractatus Canonicus de Matrimonio*, 2 vol., *Editio tertia*, Parisiis 1904.

GENICOT, EDUARDUS, *Institutiones Theologiae Moralis, Editio decima* (*Tertia post Codicem Juris Canonici*), 2 vol., Bruzellis 1922.

GURY, P. IOANNES PETRUS, *Compendium Theologiae Moralis*, 2 vol., *Editio Romana*, Romae 1873.

HASTINGS, *Dictionary of the Apostolic Church*, New York 1909.

HASTINGS, *Encyclopedia of Religion and Ethics*, New York 1914.

HEFELE-LECLERCQ, *Histoire des Conciles*, Paris 1910. (Hef.-Lecq.)

HEFELE-TAUNTON, *History of the Councils of the Church*, Edinburgh 1895. (Hef.-T.)

HURTER, H., *Theologiae Dogmaticae Compendium, Editio sexta aucta et emendata*, Oeniponte 1889.

KIRCH, CONRAD, *Enchiridion Fontium Historiae Ecclesiasticae Antiquae, Editio secunda et tertia, aucta et emendata*, Friburgi Brisgoviae 1914.

Katschthaler, Ioannes, *Theologia Dogmatica Catholica Specialis*, Ratisbonae 1884.

Knoll, *Institutiones Theologiae Theoreticae*, Editio VII, Augustae Taurinorum 1883.

La Croix, Claudius, *Theologia Moralis, Editio novissima*, Coloniae 1739.

Leech, George Leo, *A Comparative Study of The Constitution "Apostolicae Sedis" and the "Codex Juris Canonici,"* Washington 1922.

Lehmkuhl, Augustinus, *Theologia Moralis, Editio Tertia*, Friburgi Brisgoviae 1886, (also edition 1914).

Lugo, Card. Ioannes de, *Opera*, Venetiis 1751.

Mansi, *Amplissima Collectio Conciliorum*, Parisiis 1901-1913.

Minge, *Patrologia Graeca*, (MPG).

Minge, *Patrologia Latina*, (MPL).

Motry, Hubert Louis, *The Concept of Mortal Sin in Early Christianity*, Washington 1920.

Noldin, H., *Summa Theologiae Moralis*, III, *De Sacramentis, Editio decima tertia*, Oeniponte 1920.

Otten, Bernard, *Manual of the History of Dogmas*, St. Louis 1917.

Pallavicini, P. Sforza, *Histoire du Concile de Trente*, III, Montrouge 1844.

Perin, *Tractatus de Sacramento Baptismi*, Lovanii 1777.

Perrone, Ioannes, *Praelectiones Theologicae*, vol. I, *Editio* XXXVI, Ratisbonae 1881.

Pesch, Christianus, *Praelectiones Theologia Dogmaticae*, VI, *Editio quarta*, Friburgi Brisgoviae 1914, VII, *Editio quarta et quinta*, Friburgi Brisgoviae 1920.

Pourrat, P., *Theology of the Sacraments*, authorized translation from the third French edition, St. Louis 1910.

Prummer, D. M., *Manuale Juris Canonici, Editio tertia, aucta et secundum recentissimas decisiones Romanas recognita*, Friburgi Brisgoviae 1922.

Prummer, D. M., *Manuale Moralis Theologiae*, III, *Editio altera et tertia aucta et secundum novum codicem juris canonici recognita*, Friburgi Brisgoviae 1923.

REUTER, LEHMKUHL, UMBERG, *Neo-Confessarius, Editio tertia,* Friburgi Brisgoviae 1919.

Rituale Romanum, editio typica, Ratisbonae et Romae 1913.

ROUET DE JOURNAL, M. J., *Enchiridion Patristicum,* (R. de J.), *Editio quarta et quinta,* Friburgi Brisgoviae 1922.

SABETTI, ALOYSIUS-BARRETT, TIMOTHEUS, *Compendium Theologiae Moralis, Editio vicessima septima,* Neo Eboraci 1919.

SUAREZ, R. P. FRANCISCUS, *Opera Omnia, Editio nova, a Carolo Berton, tom. vigesimus,* Parisiis 1860.

TANQUEREY, AD., *Synopsis Theologiae Moralis et Pastoralis, editio septima,* Romae 1920.

THOMAS, ST., *Summa Theologica, editio altera Romana,* Romae 1894.

VACANT-MANIGNOT, *Dictionnaire de Theo. Cath.,* Paris 1920.

VERMEERSCH, A., *Theologia Moralis,* III, Mechliniae-Romae 1923.

VERMEERSCH, A.-CREUSEN, J., *Epitome Juris Canonici,* 3 vols., I, Mechliniae-Romae 1921, II, 1922, III, 1923.

VERMEERSCH, A., translated by Page, W. Humphrey, *Tolerance,* London 1913.

VIGOUROUX, *Dictionnaire de la Bible,* Paris 1912.

VLAMING, TH. M., *Praelectiones Juris Matrimonii, tertio edidit,* Bussum in Hollandia 1921.

WATKINS, O. D., *A History of Penance,* vol. I, London 1920.

CHAPTER I.

THE TERMS, THEIR HISTORY AND SIGNIFICATION.

The history of the terms "heresy" and "schism" is of some little interest to the student of Canon Law. In the present chapter, however, the growth in content and the distinction between them are alone the object of investigation. The significance of the terms *infidelis*, *haereticus*, and *schismaticus*, which are found in the Code, is of considerable importance.

1. *History of the Terms.*[1]

Christianity naturally, at least in the early period, used the terms in vogue at the time to express religious ideas. The two words *hairesis* and *schisma* are obviously Greek. "Heresy" in profane usage designated "a philosophical school of thought," and hence "a sect."[2] "Schism" simply meant "a tear" or "a rent" in a garment.[3] It is clear, then, that neither term had any religious signification, nor any note of opprobrium attached. The transition in Christian times was easy and natural.

Writers in encyclopedias note a gradual growth in the connotation of the term "heresy" from "a party, or a school," to a group of persons teaching and believing positive error, which is absolutely condemned.[4] Finally, they find "heresy" as an organization—the Nicolaitians.[5] The word "schism" is used at first in

1 Cfr. *The Catholic Encyclopedia,* articles "Heresy," "Schism." Vacant-Manignot, *Dictionnaire de Theologie Catholique.* Vigouroux, *Dictionnaire de la Bible.* Non-Catholic: Hastings, *Encyclopedia of Religion and Ethics;* Hastings, *Dictionary of the Apostolic Church.*

2 Cfr. Encyclopedia articles, and also etymological definitions given by Tertullian (*De Prae. Haer.*, VI, MPL, 2, 18), and St. Jerome (*In Galat.*, VI, MPL, 26, 417, c. 27, C. XXIV, q. 3).

3 Cfr. Encyclopedia articles "Schism."

4 Cfr. Encyclopedia articles "Heresy."

5 Apocalypse, II, 6: cfr. I Jo., I, 1-3; II, 18; IV, 2-6.

the Sacred Scriptures in its primitive meaning,[6] but is considered by the same authorities to designate in the hands of St. Paul "a party strife within the Church, closely connected with heresy."[7]

The Apostolic Fathers condemn error and its leaders in vivid terms.[8] It is clearly a very serious matter, but its members can be prayed for, and with difficulty repent.[9] Heresy, in this age, seems to have comprised a main leader with a coterie of followers, without any very definite organization, but outside of the Church.

The Fathers of the Apostolic Age sharply distinguish from these a second class, characterized not by false belief, but disciplinary strife within the fold. It is evidently less serious, as repentance is much easier, and strong epithets are not applied. It is essentially a difference of opinion with authority, not necessarily on doctrinal grounds, the adherents of which unlike heretics remain within the Church.[10]

In the Post-Apostolic Period, it would seem that organization of heretical bodies as religious sects has become a reality, as St. Irenaeus says that their mem-

6 Matthew IX, 16; Mark II, 21.

7 I Cor., I, 10; XI, 18. Cfr. Vigouroux, l. c., who states the Greek commentators did not find the distinction between heresy and schism in these passages; Vacant-Manignot, op. c., contends that they did.

8 Cfr. Encyclopedia, l. c., Louis Motry, *The Concept of Mortal Sin in Early Christianity*, p. 17-19.

9 Cfr. Motry, op. c., l. c., who opposes the sterner view taken by Rauschen, *Eucharist and Penance*, p. 183. Motry cites St. Ignatius *Ad Philad.*, III, 2, and refers to Dionysius of Corinth and Clement of Alexandria for the third century. St. Polycarp, *Ad Philad.*, VI, 1 (R. de J., No. 73), urges the presbyters to be merciful to all, and not severe in judgment, "scientes nos omnes debitores esse peccati." The views of the Shepherd of Hermas are admittedly obscure, but he seems to call on heretics to repent (Hermas, III, Simil. 8, 6; MPG, 2, 975-978). Cfr. Otten, *Manual of the History of Dogmas*, p. 93-96.

10 *Didache*, XV, 2 (R. de J., No. 9), warns the faithful to constitute "episcopos et diaconos," with the added injunction "Ne igitur contemnatis eos." Pope Clement, *Ep. ad Cor.*, I, XLIX, 2 (R. de J., No. 26), LIV, 2 (MPG, 1, 298-230), contains a description of schism, LVII, 2 (MPG, 1, 324), uses a synonym. *Ep. Barnabas*, XIX, 12 (R. de J., No. 37), "Non facies schisma. . . . Non accedes ad orationem in conscientia mala."

bers should not offer oblations,[11] Tertullian refers to the baptisms given by Marcion,[12] and Clement of Alexandria argues that heretics have arid sacraments.[13] The beginnings also of a distinction between the crime and the sin of heresy are evident, e.g., in St. Irenaeus,[14] Tertullian,[15] and Hippolytus.[16] A clear distinction in fact and treatment is drawn between the simple or "mild," and the agents of Satan or "fierce" by St. Irenaeus,[17] Tertullian,[18] and Hippolytus.[19] Probably this is the germ from which grew the theological distinction between a formal and a material heretic.

The difference between heresy and schism is not completely lost sight of by the writers of this period, such as St. Irenaeus,[20] and Hippolytus.[21] St. Cyprian expressly discussed the relation of the Church to schism, and clearly distinguished it from heresy, in combatting the Novations.[22] His views are, however, very strict. The spirit of compromise between the Pope and St. Cyprian, although he seemed to be regarded as at least a schismatic by the Pope, the canons concerning schism in the first council of Arles (314), and the difference in treatment of the schismatical Miletans, as compared with the heretical Arians, by the first ecumenical council of Nice (325), show clearly that there was a practical distinction drawn between heresy and schism.

---

11 *Adv. Haer.*, IV, 18, 4 (R. de J., No. 234). Cfr. St. Ignatius, *Ad Smy.*, VII, 1 (R. de J., No. 64), "Ab eucharistia et oratione abstinent," which is obviously not yet performed outside the Christian community.

12 *Adv. Marcionem*, IV, 9 (MPL, 2, 368).

13 *Stromata*, I, 19 (MPG, 8, 813).

14 *Adv. Haer.*, I, 16, 3 (MPG, 7, 634-635).

15 *De Prae. Haer.*, XVI (MPL, 2, 29).

16 *Contra Noetum*, I (MPG, 10, 803-806).

17 *Adv. Haer.*, IV, 26, 2 (MPG, 7, 1053); III, 15, 2 (MPG, 7, 886).

18 *Apol.*, XXXIX (MPL, 1, 471).

19 *Refutation*, VIII, 1 and 12 (ANF, V, p. 117, 133-134). (This is, however, possibly not the work of this author.)

20 *Adv. Haer.*, IV, 33, 7 (R. de J., No. 242).

21 *Refutation*, VIII, 1 and 12 (ANF, V, l. c.).

22 *De Unitate*, III (CSEL, III, 1, p. 211-212); VI (CSEL, l. c., p. 213-214); VII-X (CSEL, l. c., p. 215-219).

It was not, however, until the time of St. Augustine (354-430), St. Jerome (342-419), and St. Optatus (circa 370), that technical theological clarity of definition and distinction became pronounced. Their formulae and distinctions were later incorporated in the *Decretum Gratiani.* St. Augustine gave the element of formal culpability a prominent place in his definition of heresy: "Qui sententiam suam, quamvis falsam atque perversam, nulla pertinaci animositate defendunt, praesertim quam non audacia suae praesumptionis pepererunt, sed a seductis atque in errorem lapsis parentibus acceperunt, quaerunt autem cauta sollicitudine veritatem, corrigi parati, cum invenerint, nequaquam sunt inter haereticos deputandi."[23] St. Jerome's is descriptive, but does not necessarily contain this element.[24] Schism is also clearly defined,[25] and distinguished from heresy,[26] which St. Jerome expresses thus: "Inter haeresim et schisma hoc esse arbitramur, quod haeresis perversum dogma habeat; schisma propter episcopalem dissentionem ab Ecclesia separatur."[27] It is also clearly stated that heresy is more sinful than schism.

The definitions of St. Augustine and St. Jerome are found in the *Decretum Gratiani* (1140-1150).[29] In the Decretals of Gregory IX (1234) and the *Liber Sextus* of Boniface VIII (1298) the formal and external elements are stressed, as the canonical rather than the theological definition are the main consideration.

---

23 *Ep.*, XLII, 1: MPL, 33, 159; c. 29, C. XXIV, q. 3.

24 *In ep. ad Titum*, MPL, 26, 598; *ad Gal.*, MPL, 26, 417. c. 27, C. XXIV, q. 3.

25 St. Augustine, *Contra Faustum*, 20, 3.

26 E. g., St. Augustine, *Contra Cres. Don.*, 2, 3-7, MPL, 43, 471, cfr. Vacant-Manignot, op. c., "Heresie": *De Bapt. contra Don.*, 5, 16, MPL, 43, 186-187. St. Jerome, *In Ep. ad Titum*, 3, 10; c. 26, C. XXIV, q. 3. St. Optatus, *De sch. Don.*, 7, 3, 8; MPL, 11.

27 *In Ep. ad Titum*, 26, 598.

28 St. Optatus, *De Schism. Don.*, 1, 3, 28, MPL, 11, 891.

29 Cfr. cs. 26, 27, 28, 30, 31, C. XXIV, q. 3.

St. Thomas probably completed the process of exactness of distinction and definition of the terms. Schism is a lesser sin than heresy, because "haeresis se habet per additionem ad schisma: addit enim perversum dogma."[31] Schism is of a twofold nature, in so far as: "Ecclesiae autem unitas in duobus attenditur; scilicet: in connexione membrorum Ecclesiae ad invicem, seu communicatione; et iterum in *ordine* omnium membrorum Ecclesiae ad unum caput, . . . et ideo schismatici dicuntur, qui subesse renuunt summo Pontifici et qui membris Ecclesiae ei subjectis communicare recusant."[32] These two types of schism are embraced and distinguished in the definition of a schismatic found in the Code.[33]

The definition of papal infallibility by the Vatican Council (1869)[34] did not destroy the distinction between heresy and schism. But since the denial of a dogma of faith involves heresy, schism often includes heresy.[35]

2. *The Terms in the Code.*

There are three terms used in the Code, descriptive of the three general classes of non-Catholics—in our sense of the term—*infidelis*, *haereticus*, and *schismaticus.*

1. *Infidelis.*

The fundamental mark of division is the reception of Baptism. All those who do not possess this primary requisite fall under the general class-name *infidelis.*

30 cs. 9, 10, X, *De Haereticis,* V, 7. (Throughout the title, the emphasis is on the crime of heresy, and avoidance of contagion and penalties.) The second title of fifth book of the *Liber Sextus* of Boniface VIII contains twenty chapters *De Haereticis* in relation to the external forum, e. g., the duties of inquisitors, the goods of heretics, etc.

31 *Summa,* II-II, q. xxxix, a. 2, *sed contra.*

32 *Summa,* II-II, q. xxxix, a. 1, *respondeo.*

33 Canon 1325, no. 2.

34 Sess. IV, cap. 4.

35 Vermeersch-Creusen, *Epitome Juris Canonici* (cited in the future chapters simply "Vermeersch-Creusen"), III, no. 513.

As far as the administration of the Sacraments is concerned in the case of the dying, the fact that they are unbaptized is the essential consideration. They are neither members nor subjects of the Church. Many subdivisions could be introduced within this class, but the class and not the species is the primary concern.

2. *Haereticus.*

A heretic is one, who after the reception of Baptism, retaining the name of Christian, pertinaciously denies or doubts any of the truths that must be believed on divine or Catholic faith.[37]

This canon uses the term *pertinax,* and so the definition is of a *formal* heretic. He must be baptized, and internally or externally deny or doubt one or more of the articles of faith, but continue a Christian in name. Denial and doubt can be indifferently mental states, and the subject pertinacious in his adherence, without necessarily giving external expression to it.[38] Obviously, this mental state will have to be externalized in some way, that cognizance be taken of it in the external forum. But there are canons in the Code which concern the internal forum, in which the term occurs.[39] The term *pertinaciter,* as used in the Constitution *Apostolicae Sedis* and the past definitions of heresy, has always, according to the common interpretation of theologians, involved elements of bad faith.

The *crime* of heresy demands further conditions. A crime, in the sense of Canon Law, presupposes an external and morally imputable violation of the law, to which an at least indeterminate canonical sanction is attached.[40] This also postulates a formal mortal sin.[41]

36 Canon 87.
37 Canon 1325, no. 2.
38 Blat, *Commentarium,* III, Pars IV, p. 242: contra, Vermeersch-Creusen, II, no. 660, who inserts the word *externe* in the definition.
39 E. g., cs. 731, no. 2, 2314.
40 Canon 2195, no. 1.
41 Canon 2314, no. 2.

But the crime involves the incurrence of the censure,[42] which in turn requires some contumacy.[43] The Church does not judge the occult in her external forum, so that all heretics and schismatics are, due to the very state in which they were, presumed to fall under the censure of canon 2314. It is clear that they are or have been in a public state of defection from the Church, and have performed acts in accordance with this state. The public forum of the Church can only judge, in the absence of proof to the contrary, that the intention follows the act. Hence, ignorance of the law is not presumed,[44] and so long as the positive external violation of the law has taken place, regardless of purely internal conditons, *dolus* is presumed in the external forum, until the contrary is proved.[45] Hence, there is a *praesumptio juris* that the crime is there and is morally imputable. The excommunication in canon 2314 is juridically incurred *ipso facto,* until the contrary is proven.

There is a difference betwen the sin and the crime of heresy. The latter always involves the former, but the contrary is not true. Thus, the sin of heresy is committed by entertaining in bad faith a serious doubt regarding an article of faith, although this may be made manifest to others in no way whatsoever. As soon as the party gives expression to this, and the necessary *contumacy* is had, the canonical crime of heresy, with the consequent censure, is incurred. The present canon, then, embraces both the crime and the sin, the external and the internal state of formal heresy.

These distinctions are of great importance in determining the licit practice to be followed. But where there is question of the administration of the Sacra-

42 Canon 2314, no. 1.
43 Canon 2241, no. 1, cfr. 2242.
44 Canon 2202, no. 1.
45 Canon 2200, no. 2.

ments, the widest possible use of the term is employed, embracing all heretics, "etiam bona fides petentibus," guilty of the sin and the crime, or the sin alone, formal or material.[46] This canon also gives additional ground for the distinction between formal and material heretics, although the process to be followed before admitting them to the Sacraments is the same.

3. *Schismaticus.*

A schismatic is also a baptized person. The precise point of difference is that he rejects the Supreme Pontiff or refuses to communicate with the members of the Church subject to him.[47] Schism violates the unity of the Church, either in the relation of the members to the head, or the connection of the members among themselves.[48] This section of the canon, then, is an epitome of the teaching of the Angelic Doctor. If the schism involves a denial of the supremacy of jurisdiction of the Pope, or his prerogative of infallibility, it is known as heretical schism. This is not, however, necessarily the case, so that pure schism, which is not also heretical, is possible.

As far as the administration of the Sacraments is concerned, the same distinctions as have been made in the case of a heretic can be applied.[49]

---

46 Canon 731, no. 2.

47 Canon 1325, no. 2.

48 Cfr. Blat., op. c., III, Pars IV, p. 243; Vermeersch-Creusen, III, no. 513, 2.

49 Cfr. canons 731, no. 2, 2314, no. 1.

CHAPTER II.

PRELIMINARY CONSIDERATIONS.

There are three fundamental problems that may confront the priest in his ministrations to dying non-Catholics, and which will underlie the concession or denial of the Sacraments in all cases. The answer that he can secure under the circumstances will to a large extent also determine which of the Sacraments can be administered. They are:

1. Who is an adult, in years and reason, relative to Baptism?
2. What attitude must be adopted towards doubtfully baptized non-Catholics in their dying moments?
3. How is the intention of the non-Catholic to be judged, and what action can be taken where there is destitution of the senses?

These three questions are of much practical moment. Their discussion, however, in the abstract, is difficult, owing to the fact that the particular circumstances of each individual case differ.

1. *Who Is the Adult?*

In canon 88, par. 3, a general presumption is stated: *expleto autem septennio, usum rationis habere praesumitur.* But in the case of Baptism, the divine law demands that another test be applied: "He that *believeth* and is baptized, shall be saved: but he that believeth not shall be condemned.[1]" The mission of the Church involves teaching: "Going therefore, *teach* ye all nations; baptizing them in the name of the Father, and of the Son, and of the Holy Ghost."[2] Now, those

1 Mark XVI, 16.
2 Matthew XXVIII, 19; cfr. Mark XVI, 15.

possessing the use of reason, regardless of their age, are capable of being taught, more or less fully in accordance with their intellectual capacity. Hence, when there is question of Baptism, they are considered as adults who enjoy the use of reason.[3] They then are subject to the conditions laid down in canon 752.

The general rule is that all, even though dying, must satisfy this canon, in so far as this is possible. But in cases of doubt, and where the circumstances do not permit of further investigation, the general presumption can be a safe basis for action, namely, if the dying subject has not completed the seventh year, he is to be treated as an infant.

The ultimate test, however, is not the age, but the presence or absence of the use of reason. This naturally flows from the necessity of fulfilling canon 752 in so far as possible. Hence, there is an express exception to the law, which may involve an extension or limitation of the age. When there is question of Baptism, canon 745 regulates:

1. Those who have not yet attained the use of reason, and among them are grouped *amentes ab infantia,* no matter of what age, come under the name of *parvuli* or *infantes,* according to the norm of canon 88, par. 3.
2. Adulti autem censentur, qui rationis usu fruuntur; idque satis est ut suo quisque animi motu baptismum petat et ad illum admittatur.

The canon referred to states that an *impubes,* before the use of reason, is called *infans seu puer vel parvulus* and considered as not being *sui compos;* after the completion of the seventh year, he is presumed to have the use of reason. Whoever is habitually destitute of the use of reason is assimilated to infantes.[4] The term

3 Canon 745, no. 2.
4 Canon 88, no. 3.

used by the canon in question *censetur* postulates presumption and not absolute certainty, which indicates that even after the seventh year, the use of reason is only presumed. But presumption must yield to fact, and the specific case will have to be judged on this basis. Thus, an extension and contraction of the age are conceded: its presence, even below the age of seven, imposes the obligations, and its absence above this age withdraws the obligations.[5]

The real difficulty arises in determining what is meant by the possession of the use of reason. It is obviously much less than is normally required for other actions. An Instruction of the Propaganda, April 17, 1777, gives much practical guidance.[6] It directly concerns *amentes* and children of four or five years, who either certainly or doubtfully perceive the principal mysteries of faith. The ultimate test given is, that they know the difference between good and evil, and be capable of sinning, (*culpae se reos reddere valeant*).

2. *The General Attitude Towards Doubtful Baptism.*

The growing disregard of the Sacrament of Baptism among the non-Catholics of the United States is an undeniable fact. It is likewise a fact of common observation that the ministers of non-Catholic sects oftentimes neglect or fail to observe all the conditions required for administering valid Baptism. European theologians have noted this, and some consider all Baptisms by non-Catholics in the United States as probably invalid. If this could be established as an *actual* custom, past responses of the Holy Office would admit it as a general presumption, capable of being acted on in the absence of proof to the contrary. But American theologians do not admit any such sweeping

5 Capello, *De Sacramentis,* I, no. 153.
6 Ad II, Coll., no. 522.

statement.[7]

An investigation must be made in each individual case, even in the circumstances of approaching death, in regard to both the fact and the validity of a possible previous Baptism.[8] It is clear that the thoroughness of such an investigation must be largely determined by the circumstances. The testimony of one witness *omni exceptione maior,* or the baptized person himself under oath, if he received Baptism as an adult, is sufficient to prove the fact of Baptism.[9] With this proven, the priest must then proceed to investigate the validity of this previous Baptism, in which his own pastoral experience will be the best guide. Two dogmas must be respected: first, valid Baptism must not be repeated;[10] and, secondly, anyone can baptize validly who satisfies the conditons.[11] Hence, the Code states the general law

---

7 St. Alphonsus (*Theologia Moralis,* VI, no. 137), gives a general principle that all are to be rebaptized conditionally in case they have been previously baptized *a praedicantibus.* But this could not be done without investigation, as the Instruction of the Holy Office, November 20, 1878, which is typical, requires investigation in each individual case (ASS, XI, p. 613-615). Some authors postulate an actual custom of invalidly baptizing among non-Catholics of the United States, e. g., Lehmkuhl (*Theologia Moralis,* II, note to no. 26, Ed. XII, 1914), Vermeersch Creusen (II, no. 38), seems to admit Lehmkuhl's view, Genicot (*Institutiones Theologiae Moralis,* II, p. 137, nota). Capello, *De Sacramentis,* I, no. 174), notes that this view "nonnisi cum debita discretione accipiendum esse arbitramur." Sabetti-Barrett (American), (*Theologia Moralis,* p. 583), contains a table of the different sects, which bears out Lehmkuhl's view for Episcopalians, Methodists, Presbyterians, Congregationalists, Unitarians, Universalists, Baptists, Socinians, and Quakers, but rejects it for Oriental heretics and Old Catholics.

Past responses of the Holy See have taken the *actual* custom of baptizing invalidly as a safe presumption of invalidity, e. g., Instr. S. C. de Prop. Fide, June 23, 1830, Col., no. 814, in fine, S. C. S. Off., November 17, 1830, ad 3, Coll., no. 821 (. . . *nullum baptismum ex consuetudine actuali illius sectae* . . .), Instr. S. C. de Prop. Fidei, July 26, 1845, Coll., no. 999 (. . . *non est imprudens nec insuetum, propter haereticorum incertam et suspectam praxim* . . .), S. C. S. Off., July 5, 1853, ad 3, Coll., no. 1096 (. . . *ex consuetudine actuali eiusdem sectae* . . .), etc.

8 The responses of the Holy Office make no distinction between investigation in the case of the healthy and the dying, e. g., Instruction, Holy Office, November 20, 1878 (ASS, XI, p. 613-615).

9 Canon 779.

10 Trent, Sess. VII, *De Baptismo,* can. 11, 13, 14.

11 Trent, Sess. VII, *De Baptismo,* can. 4. (The precise object of this dogmatic canon is a heretic baptizing.)

that if there is a prudent doubt whether the Baptism was either really or validly conferred or not, it is to be repeated conditionally.[12] An actual custom on the part of a particular non-Catholic minister, known to the priest from former investigation, will certainly give ground for a prudent doubt, if the dying person was baptized by him. But it seems to be extreme to act on a general notion that all non-Catholics baptize invalidly in the United States.

3. *Cases in Which There Is No Possibility of a Sign.*

1. *The Problem.*

It is obvious that if the dying person is in control of his senses and can communicate with the minister, sufficient investigation can be made to ascertain the nature of his intention. Further, even though he lost power of definite communication, signs both from the past and the present, either by the dying person or through others, will afford a basis for action. Such signs and cases will be investigated in subsequent chapters. But suppose there are no signs, as far as the minister is concerned, and due to destitution of the senses, no further information can be obtained from the subject or others. Can the Sacraments be administered to such a one conditionally? This is the problem. It is also understood throughout the discussion that the subject is on the point of death.

2. *Method and Object.*

It may be stated at the outset that there is and has been considerable diversity of opinions in the solution of this problem. It is particularly difficult in the case of Baptism, which forms the first division in the present section; perhaps a little less difficult in that of Penance, the second division.

The object of this discussion is to present the sub-

12 Canon 732, no. 2.

stance of the arguments urged by both opinions, offer a few suggestions, which may, without any claim whatsoever on the part of the writer to certitude, provide a new point of view, and consider the main objections. It is hoped thereby that the practical conclusions drawn may have sufficient support to warrant action.

A. The Sacrament of Baptism.

In the hypothesis nothing is known concerning the absence or presence of the intention of being baptized on the part of the subject.

1. *The Affimative.*

The opinion of Catherinus, at least as far as the minister of the Sacrament is concerned, has passed out of the schools. But the recipient of the Sacraments is the subject of the present discussion. Pope Benedict XIV in his Constitution *Postremo mense,* February 28, 1747, states that the view of Catherinus, " . . . minus habet difficultatis, cum non de conferente agatur, sed de accipiente Baptismum. Propositio autem ab Alexandro VIII damnata, objici Catherino solita, conferentem respicit, non accipientem."[13] The same Pope, however, admits in a later work that the proposition of Pope Alexander VIII inflicted a "grave vulnus" on the opinion.[14] It is today without any following, although

13 No. 47, Benedicti XIV, Bullarium, II, p. 185. The passage is as follows: "Quidquid sit de opinione Catharini, qui sustinet, conferenti exteriorem sufficere compositionem, etiam si non id animo proponat facere, quod Ecclesia solet, de qua opinione multa alibi diximus in nostro Tractatu *de Sacrificio Missae ad part. 4, sect. 2, num. 76 et seqq.* haec, inquam, opinio mimus habet difficultatis, cum non de conferente agatur, sed de accipiente Baptismum. Propositio autem ab Alexandro VIII, damnata, objici Catherino solita, conferentem respicit, non accipientem: *Valet Baptismus collatus a Ministro, qui omnem ritum externum, formamque Baptismi observat, intus vero, et in corde suo resolvit, non intendo facere, quod facit Ecclesia.*" Cfr. Pourratt, *The Theology of the Sacraments,* p. 391, who says that Pope Alexander VIII expressly declared that he was not condemning the view of Catharinus; Hurter, *Theo. Dogm. Comp.,* III, no. 337.

14 *De syn. dioc.,* VII, 4, 8, which was published in 1748, and revised and augmented 1755, refers expressly to the *Postremo mense,* Lib. VI, cap. 4. But Pallavicini, *Historie du Concile de Trente* (cited in future

it can hardly be said to have received special attention from viewpoint of the recipient expressly. The well-known neutral view of Cardinal Cajetan, although not common, has some force. Possibly Lehmkuhl refers to these theologians, and accepts their opinions as sufficient ground in our hypothesis for the conditional administration of Baptism.

Another class of theologians consider that an act of sorrow *ex fide concepta habent pro voluntate baptismi fortasse sufficienti.*[15] Some who reject this view concede that it can be acted on in our hypothesis.[16]

Still another theologian, admitting some slight probability in the former opinion, permits conditional Baptism, because of the salvific will of Christ.[17]

Thus, it would seem, in our humble judgment, that the affirmative opinion has but slight intrinsic foundation from viewpoint of intention, although it has sufficient extrinsic probability for the conditional administration of Baptism in the hypothesis.

2. *The Negative.*

At the opposite extreme are found very eminent theo-

---

references simply Pallavicini), IX, 6, no. 2, 3, expressly relates that the Fathers of this Council purposely avoided condemning the view of Catharinus.

15 Cfr. Lehmkuhl, op. c., II, no. 78 (Ed. 3, 1886); Vermeersch-Creusen, II, no. 35; Genicot, *Inst. Theo. Mor.*, II, no. 150; Capello, *De Sacramentis,* I, no. 155, does not reject the view because of its extrinsic probability, and in our particular hypothesis, as a practical conclusion, says: "Palam est Baptismum esse conferendum sub conditione." Pesch, *Tract. Dogm.*, VI, no. 439, rejects the view of Suarez for practice, with the restriction noted in our practical conclusions, on the ground that the intention cannot be fixed theoretically.

Prümmer, *Man. Theo. Mor.*, III, no. 135, seems to maintain that Baptism cannot be given without a positive presumption. A large group of theologians analyze the least possible intention that will satisfy for validity, and from this conclude that the negative opinion is proved. In our humble opinion, which we believe is that of Pesch, l. c., Lehmkuhl, l. c., Genicot, l. c., this does not touch the real question, as the possibility of *licit* administration of conditional Baptism under the circumstances and not its valid reception is the question. From the very nature of the case, nothing can be known concerning the validity or invalidity until the subject manifests his mind.

16 Cfr. Capello, l. c., Lehmkuhl, l. c., Genicot, l. c.

17 Genicot, l. c.

logians, such as Suarez and Lugo. They demand absolutely an intention for the reception of Baptism, and consequently conclude that it cannot be conferred without a sign in the present hypothesis. The arguments presented by the adherents of this view are usually as follows:

1. A refutation of the affirmative opinions;
2. A statement that in cases in which there is no knowledge of the intention of the subject, the Church presumes the contrary;[18]

---

18 Suarez, *Opera Omnia,* vol. 30, D. XIV, sec. 2, no. 4. S. Bonaventurae, *Opera Omnia,* Tom. IV (Quaracchi, 1889), Sent. Lib. IV, D. IV., P. I, art. 2, q. 1, p. 101 (Conclusio), 3: "Ad illud quod obiicitux, quod Sacramentum est donum Dei; dicendum, quod est donum gratiae gratis datae et gratum facientis; quamvis autem donum gratiae gratum facientis non detur habenti duplex cor et duplicem voluntatem, datur tamen donum gratiae gratis datae, *quod non exigit tantam dispositionem in suscipiente.*" 4: "Ad illud quod obiicitur, quod lex evangelica est lex libertatis; dicendum, quod verum est, quod de *iure* non datur nec dari debet ei qui libera voluntate non accedit; et ius divinum hoc dictat, et Constantinus de hoc legem condidit. De *facto* tamen, si fiat, factum est; hoc tamen habet veritatem in re Sacramenti, quod facit esse in lege libertatis." "3. 4. Ad illud quod obiicitur ultimo de comminatione mortis; dicendum, quod maior potest esse coactio quam haec; nam haec est solum *inducens,* non sufficiens. Sed *cum* accipitur, velit nolit, et immergitur, ibi est *sufficiens* coactio. Quamvis enim voluntas non possit cogi *in volendo,* potest tamen simpliciter homini fieri coactio *in actu exteriori.* Unde voluntas *inducta* voluntas est; et ideo hic imprimitur character, et ibi non. Et est exemplum in eo qui ponit thura timore mortis, et de eo cuius manus trahitur violenter; primus consentit et peccat et dicitur *sacrificare,* secundus non. Sic qui Sacramentum *inductus* suscipit, consentire; sive inducatur amore bono vel malo, sive timore bono vel malo, suscipit Sacramentum, quia Sacramentum susceptio est bonis malisve communis. Et ideo talis voluntas sufficit ad Sacramentum, ut seniores dicunt. Et sic patet, quibus character baptismalis imprimitur."

Joannis Duns Scoti, *Opera Omnia,* Tom. XVI (Parisiis, 1894), Lib. IV, Sent., D. IV, q. 4, Scholium, p. 417: (In regard to adults, who "aut non utitur nunc ratione, sed aliquando est usus"): "Sed, expeditne talem baptizari? Multa enim licet, quae non expediunt, 1 Corinth. 6. Respondeo, si speretur eum rediturum ad usum rationis, magis expedit tempus expectare, quo uteretur ratione, puta de dormiente, tempus vigiliae expedit expectare, et de furioso tempus lucidi intervalli. Si autem non speretur, puta de eo, qui incidit in perpetum impedimentum usus rationis, eum expedit baptizare, si tamen est capax Baptismi, quia alias exponeretur periculo damnationis. Qualiter autem sit capax, statim dicetur de utente ratione." Scholium, p. 420: "Et esto quod sic, numquid ille, qui tantum negative non consentit, negative etiam non dissentit? quia nec actum, nec habitum oppositum habet. De primo posset dici, quod talis judicatur habitualiter consentiens, quia aliquando habuit consensum actualem, non interveniente dissensu; et talis, licet utens ratione, recipit Sacramentum, quia non videtur propter aliquam condi-

3. Christ does not want Baptism imposed on anyone against his will;[19]
4. The acceptance of a gift and a new life demands a volitional human act.[19]

The first argument does not necessarily prove that the present view (negative) is correct, but it does establish a greater probability. The second argument is

---

tionem minus capax, si utitur ratione, quam si prius usus, non utatur nunc; sed in tali non utente nunc, prius tamen uso, sufficeret habitualis consensus; ergo et hic. De secundo, licet, difficile esset aliquem talem invenire, praecipue qui prius aliquando cogitasset de Baptismo, quia vel tunc placuisset, imo displicuisset, et secundum ultimum modum judicaretur talis habitualis consensus vel dissensus esse in posterum, tamen si quis esset omnino non consentiens, nec dissentiens, tam actualiter quam habitualiter, et tamen utens ratione, non esset capax Baptismi, quia ex quo utitur ratione, oportet quod habeat devotionem aliquam ad Sacramentum, si debet sibi valere, aliter enim videretur contemnere."

The following passage from the *Summa* of St. Thomas, which is extremely disputed, seems, in the humble opinion of the writer, to agree with the above citations: (III, q. 64, a. 8, *ad secundum*) "Sed hoc satis posset dici, quantum ad ultimum effectum, qui est justificatio a peccatis; sed quantum ad effectum, qui est res, et sacramentum, scilicet quantum ad characterem, non videtur quod per devotionem accedentis possit suppleri: quia character numquam imprimitur, nisi per sacramentum; et ideo alii melius dicunt, quod minister sacramenti agit in persona totius Ecclesiae, cujus est minister; *in verbis* autem, quae profert, *exprimitur intentio Ecclesiae; quae* sufficit ad perfectionem sacramenti *nisi contrarium exterius* exprimatur ex parte ministri, *vel recipientis sacramentum.*"

Cajetan concluded that a neutral intention would suffice for validity, which intention Suarez rejected. Possibly a compromise could be made, the lack of an expressed contrary will suffices for licit administration in extreme cases *in faciem Ecclesiae,* the validity *per se* being judged by the principles laid down by the Angelic Doctor for the *perfection* of the Sacrament: "Ad tertium dicendum, quod licet ille qui aliud cogitat, non habeat actualem intentionem, habet tamen intentionem habitualem, quae sufficit ad *perfectionem sacramenti.* . . ."

The crux of the question seems to be: What will suffice for the licit administration? The validity will naturally be determined by the actual possession of some intention, and the Sacrament *post factum* will be judged on a basis of the content of this intention or its *actual* absence, not the knowledge of it by the minister.

19 Katschtaler, *Theo. Dogm.*, IV, no. 154. Two further practical objections are urged. Canon 1351 reads: "Ad amplexandam fidem catholicam nemo invitus cogatur." In the footnotes to this canon reference is made to canons 752 and 754, which regulate the administration of Baptism in extreme cases, where the right of the person, even though *in extremis,* is guarded by the demand of manifested intention. Doctors and psychologists also state that oftentimes dying persons, who are unable in any manner to communicate with bystanders, continue to be conscious of what is going on around them. Hence, if the dying person did not want the ministrations of a priest, it is quite possible that his good faith would be changed into bad faith. Sometimes another objection is raised which really has not practical foundation, in our humble opinion, namely, the danger of religious indifferentism.

not very serious when the salvation of a soul is at stake. The third and fourth are not as one supposes the presence of the intention (3) and the other its absence (4).

If the knowledge of the subject's intention, in addition to its possession, were clearly proven by the defenders of this view to be necessary for licit conditional administration in our hypothesis, in the humble opinion of the writer, the case would be solved. This seems to be the weakest link in the whole opinion and discussion.

3. *A Few Suggestions.*

The real difficulty is perhaps not the lack of intention, which is unknown, but the lack of knowledge. Hence, the Baptism administered cannot be declared certainly valid or invalid until the facts are known with the recovery of the subject.

Lack of knowledge in regard to a condition required for validity in some cases at least permits of conditional repetition or administration of Baptism, e.g., a fetus,[20] a *monstrum,*[21] a foundling,[22] etc.

If an act of sorrow "*ex fide concepta*" can be postulated, it is hard to see that God's assistance must necessarily stop short at this. Consequently, some theologians [23] teach that it passes into a perfect act of contrition. If this be the case, then, at least some kind of *votum Baptismi* is present.

4. *Practical Conclusions.*

In the abstract, it would seem, intrinsically the problem has not found adequate solution. Extinsically, the milder opinion seems to have sufficient support for action. The case, however, as it occurs is hardly ca-

20 Canon 747.
21 Canon 748.
22 Canon 749.
23 E.g., *St. Alphonsus, Theo. Mor.*, VI, no. 8; Lehmkuhl, l.c. Pesch, *Tract. T. Dogm.*, VI, no. 311.

pable of being finally and definitely settled in the abstract. If there are no signs, there are surely some circumstances which will aid, e.g., that the dying person is now married to a Catholic wife, or was a member of some Christian sect, or worked with Catholic companions who perhaps discussed religion, and other suchlike acts, which pastoral prudence will weigh. If there are no signs, but contrary acts, e.g., positive refusal and violation of the *cautiones,* bitter persecution of Catholics, etc., it is certainly difficult to see how prudence would permit action. If the case happens in the concrete as considered in the abstract, it seems probable that the opinions of the theologians allowing conditional Baptism can be followed. Even those who support the opposite opinion teach that less intention is required on the part of the recipient than the minister.[24] The views of Catherinus and Cajetan have never been condemned, nor those of other theologians teaching that conditional Baptism can be administered. But it is admitted that even *slight* probability can be followed in such extreme cases.[25] Finally, the question of actual validity or invalidity can only be definitely settled by the facts in the matter, which the subject alone can reveal.

24 E. g., Suarez, *Opera omnia,* vol. XX, D. XIV, sec. 2, no. 4: "Quin potius minor concursus voluntatis hujus requiritur in suscipiente quam in ministrante Sacramentum, . . ." et alii. We have purposely refrained from citing the disputed historical facts and testimonies, and also the passage of St. Thomas, *Summa,* III, q. lxiv, a. 8, *ad sec. in fine,* which both Cajetan and Suarez use, although they hold opposite views, to support their opinions. It is not out of place, however, to cite Pourrat, op. c., p. 390, on these: "The theologians who deem the interior intention necessary must interpret the text of ancient authors which go counter to their view. The insufficiency of their explanations let us frankly admit." This "insufficiency" is intensified when it is admitted that the crux of the problem is not the possession of the intention, which is *ex hypothesi* wholly unknown, but the lack of knowledge on the part of the minister of the presence or absence of it in the subject.

25 E. g., St. Alphonsus, *Theo. Mor.,* VI, no. 481; Lehmkuhl, l. c.; Genicot, op. c., II, no. 423, et alii.

B. The Sacrament of Penance.

1. *The Hypothesis.*

As in the case of Baptism, the present discussion concerns a dying non-Catholic, who has become destitute of his senses, and has not given and is at present unable to give any sign.

2. *Preliminary Considerations.*

The difficulty in regard to the lack of knowledge by the priest concerning the intention of the dying person is not so great as in the case of the unbaptized. The dying person has been baptized, so that he is really a subject of the Church, although in a state of at least material rebellion.[26] Penance is a Sacrament of the internal forum, which, according to the Council of Trent, requires the confession of sins *sicut in conscientia.*[27] In the case the person may have been a material heretic or schismatic, under which circumstances he has not committed a formal sin of heresy, for which he is guilty in conscience. If he had been a formal heretic or schismatic, this cannot be proved or presumed in the internal forum, when he is destitute of his senses. Hence, in either case, he cannot be certainly proved unworthy. But in the extreme spiritual necessity of death, canon 882 gives any priest ample power, and *per se* at least conditional absolution must be given.

There is, however, difficulty concerning the intention of the dying person. If he was a schismatic or a member of a non-Catholic sect believing in the Sacrament of Penance, there is no reason for excluding a sacramental intention. If he was not, then he probably believes in some form of confession of sins to God, or can be presumed to be at least attrite. The Holy Office, August 1, 1855, stated a presumption for contumacious

26 Canon 87.

27 Sess. XIV, *De Sac. Poen.*, cap. 5, *de confessione.*

freemasons, . . . "quemadmodum etiam in articulo mortis possunt per contritionem in Dei gratiam redire, ac *internam* cum membris mystici corporis Christi communicationem adipisci . . ."[28] In order that these contumacious persons be absolved from the censure, even after death, they must have given clear signs of repentance. Nothing is said of absolution from sin. It is the presumption, however, which concerns us here. If this act becomes perfect contrition, it contains at least an implicit desire of Penance.[29] If it remains attrition, a disposition to ask for the Sacrament of Penance is present.[30]

3. *The Difficulties.*

The real difficulty arises from another source. Many theologians teach that some sensible sign is required for the licit administration of the Sacrament, as the acts of the penitent constitute the matter, not merely *conditio sine qua non* of the Sacrament.[31] Modern Thomists, however, are willing to concede that these may be virtually contained in an internal act of sor-

---

28 Coll., no. 1116.

29 Trent, Sess. XIV, cap. 4, *de contritione,* ". . . tamen eum ad Die gratiam in sacramento poenitentiae impetrandam disponit, . . ." and as regards perfect contrition, ". . . ipsam nihilominus reconciliationem ipsi contritioni, sine sacramenti voto, quod in illa includitur, non esse abscribendam."

30 Vide 29.

31 Those who maintain a sensible sign is necessary in *all* cases, Suarez, op. c., vol. 21, D. XXIII, sec. 1, no. 13; Lugo, *De Poenitentiae,* D. XVII, sec. 3, whose views are refuted by the editor in a footnote.

Those supporting the view in the text. Lacroix, *Theo. Mor.,* VI, pars II, no. 1162; St. Alphonsus, op. c., VI, no. 482, admits conditional absolution, except in no. 483 to non-Catholics who became destitute of their senses in the actual act of grave external mortal sin; D'Annibale, *Theo. Mor.,* III, no. 317. This is the common opinion among theologians today, e. g., Billuart, *Cursus theo.,* D. VI, a. 10, VII, 2; Vermeesch, *Theo. Mor.,* III, nos. 568, 570, 599; Lehmkuhl, op. c., II, no. 514; Genicot, op. c., II, no. 423; Prummer, *M. T. M.,* III, no. 326, who devotes a paragraph to an explanation of how this opinion is more in conformity with Thomism than Scotism (no. 327); Knoll, *Inst. Theo. Theoretice seu Dogm. Polemicae,* IV, 512, no. 3, expressly accepts with the restriction of St. Alphonsus; Pesch, op. c., VII, nos. 82-86, 191, discusses the problem, starting from the premises, "Si enim confessio sensibilis requiritur solum ut condicio praevia, sacramentum existere posse videtur sine sensi-

row.[32] Modern Scotists teach that the sensible sign is not absolutely necessary.[33]

Suarez [34] and Lugo [35] urge a second difficulty: Penance involves the exercise of a judicial act by the minister, which is impossible where no sign has been given. But modern theologians, while recognizing these difficulties, urge the giving of conditional absolution.[36]

4. *Suggestions.*

Both of the difficulties urged apply with equal force to the cases of dying Catholics.

The Church never defined that a sensible sign was necessary for the validity of the Sacrament. Theologians have not proved that the knowledge of this sensible sign as distinct from its existence is necessary for the validity of the Sacrament. As a matter of fact, the the question was expressly raised in the Council of Trent, and was purposely left undetermined.[37] Moreover, the History of the Council shows conclusively that the teaching was very carefully drafted so as to be in conformity with and not condemnatory of the reconciliation theory as proposed by Andre Vega: "However celebrated doctors are to be found among the Franciscans who try to interpret their master in a sense not different from the ordinary sense. Among others is Andre Vega, the most famous of the Scotists assisting at the Council. Already four years earlier, in the volume cited, which he wrote on the decree on justification

bili confessione, dummodo objective aliqua confessio adsit. Ita saltem quidem putare videtur," and concludes that absolution is *valde dubium* even where some signs, although indefinite, have been given; Pourrat, op. c., after an historical study of the Sacraments, agrees entirely with the affirmative view.

32 E. g., Prümmer, op. c., III, no. 327.

33 Cfr. Genicot, op. c., II, no. 300; Tanquerey, *Syn. Theo. Mor., Pars Dogm.*, III, no. 164.

34 Suarez., op. c., vol. 21, D. XXIII, sec. 1, no. 13.

35 Lugo, op. c., D. XVII, sec. 3.

36 Cfr. e. g., Genicot, op. c., l. c.

37 Pallavicini, op. c., XII, c. 11, no. 9, but distinguish what Pallavicini advances as his view, and what he says the Council did.

promulgated in the sixth session, Vega set forth the opinion of Scotus in such a way that it would seem as if it presented only a verbal difficulty, and was at bottom true. According to Vega, Scotus does not deny that these acts are parts of the Sacrament *in some fashion,* but denies that they are *essential* parts. He attributes them to the Sacrament only as integral parts, according to the language of the School, and we have seen that the Council in that acted with a great deal of concern for the opinion of Scotus. It declared in the third chapter and in the fourth canon, the acts of the penitent previously cited are not parts of the Sacrament, but parts of the virtue of penance, and it explained in this third chapter above that they are called parts of the virtue of penance in so far as by divine institution they are required in the penitent for the integrity of the Sacrament and for the full and perfect remission of the sins.''[38] This view is quite clear. In the preceding chapter, the same history notes that the Fathers possibly intended to define ''attritio fit constitutum sacramentum,''[39] but did not as they did not want to end the discussion in the schools, but were content with condemning the Protestant error. Now, it matters little to our argument whether Scotus really held this view or not. The fact is that the Council did not condemn it, and consequently no private theologian can afford to overlook it completely, or deny its probability. Vega maintains that the acts of the penitent are essential to the Sacrament only to the same degree as they are necessary to the virtue of penance. But no one would deny that they can be completely internal in

38 Ibid., XII, c. 12, no. 1.

39 Ibid., XII, c. 10, no. 26, according to Pesch, op. c., VII, Pallavicini's words are: ". . . mais encore qu'elle suffit pour la réception de ce sacrament. . . ."

the case of the virtue, so that the same must be true in the case of the Sacrament.

The difficulty from viewpoint of the judicial nature of the Sacrament is somewhat more difficult to answer. The Council of Trent teaches that it must be exercised in a judicial manner by the minister.[40] This involves a guilty person, matter on which the judgment is to be passed, and a judge. But is not the matter present in some manner? The presumption is that the dying person is at least attrite. In a word, the sinner is confessing his sins to God, perhaps expressly, though not sensibly manifesting them. The minister lacks knowledge in regard to anything further, but absolves from these sins. He is thus conscious of the sinful *condition* of the dying person, and on this passes the judgment.

5. *Confirmatory Proof.*

The continuity of practice, at least in the case of dying Catholics, under the conditions postulated, provides in itself strong confirmation. Theologians in general admit that where even the vaguest sign is given, which may be indicative of the intention, there is no difficulty. Again, they raise no difficulties against the validity of the absolution where one general absolution is given to a large group of persons at the same time, in which the sensible sign is *knowable*, but in the case of very many actually unperceived by the minister. There is a parallel between all these cases and that which we are considering.

St. Augustine writes of somewhat similar cases. "Non ipsos enim ex hac vita arrha pacis exire velle debet mater Ecclesia."[41] There is no doubt that the

40 Sess. XIV, *De Poenitentia*, canon 9. Cfr. Pesch, op. c., VII, nos. 79, 69, 15, but also nos. 82-86; Hurter, *Theo. Dogm.*, III, no. 624: "Quamvis autem poenitentiae sacramentum per modum judicii sit institutum, non tamen in omnibus hujus naturam sequitur; quoadusque illud imitetur, ex praxi colligi debet"; Vermeersch, *Theo. Mor.*, III, no. 570, 599.

41 *De adult. conjug.*, 28, 35, CSEL, vol. xli, sect. v, pars iii, p. 382.

affirmative opinion is the most common among moralists today.

This practice and teaching has never been condemned by the Holy See, but rather approved by two recent decisions of the Holy Office. In neither response was any restriction placed in regard to the difficulties discussed in the schools. The first was given, July 22, 1898: "An aliquando absolvi possint schismatici materiales, qui in bona fide versantur? R. Cum scandulum nequeat vitari, Negative, praeterquam in mortis articulo; et tunc efficaciter remoto scandalo."[42] The other response is still more striking, and was given May 26, 1916: "An schismaticis in mortis articulo sensibus destitutis absolutio et extrema unctio conferri potest? R. Sub conditione (cum de intentione allisque in poenitentia ad valorem requisitis dubitari debeat) affirmative, praesertim si ex adjunctis conjicere liceat, eos *implicite* saltem errores suos rejicere, remoto tamen scandalo, manifestando scilicet adstantibus (qui id nesciant) Ecclesiam suponere eos in ultimo momento ad unitatem rediisse."[43]

6. *Practical Conclusion.*

The practice is certain in the case of Penance, and there would seem to be an obligation at least in charity of administering this Sacrament.

---

42 ASS, XXXI, p. 254.

43 Cited by Prümmer, op. c., III, p. 223, in the footnote, from *Linzer Theol. Quartalschr.*, 1916, 693, and Reuter-Lehmkuhl-Umberg, *Neo-Confessarius*, no. 203, from *Kölner Pastoralblatt*, 50 (1916), 504.

CHAPTER III.

THE BAPTISM OF DYING NON-CATHOLICS.

The signification of the term adult in reference to the Sacrament of Baptism has already been investigated in the preceding chapter.[1] This discussion forms the natural basis of division in the subject matter of the present chapter, which falls into three sections:

1. The Baptism of dying infants of non-Catholics;
2. The Baptism of dying abnormal adults;
3. The Baptism of dying adult non-Catholics.

1. *The Baptism of Dying Infants of non-Catholics.*

The object of the writer throughout is to explain the canons of the Code. Hence, the relevant canons form the first subdivision. But the Code represents the climax of a long history, which is of much interest, and provides a second subdivision. The third comprises an attempted interpretation of the canons of the Code itself, followed by a consideration of incidental questions or objections, in accordance with the demands of the subject. This order will be maintained throughout the rest of the book, in so far as possible.

A. The Canons of the Code.

The dying infants of infidel parents are the object of canon 750, par. 1:

> Infans infidelium, etiam invitis parentibus, licite baptizatur, cum in eo versatur vitae discrimine, ut prudenter praevideatur moriturus, antequam usum rationis attingat.

The correlative canon 751 provides the general rule

1 Cfr. chapter II, no. 1.

for dying infants of heretics and schismatics:

> Circa baptismum infantium duorum haereticorum aut schismaticorum, aut duorum catholicorum qui in apostasiam vel haeresim vel schisma prolapsi sint, *generatim* serventur normae in superiore canone constitutae.

B. Historical Survey.

1. *Early Express Testimonies Concerning Infants of Non-Catholics.*

The early Fathers make no distinction in their teaching on the Baptism of infants. During the ages of persecution, this would naturally be expected, as their works were often read by pagans and heretics, and in some cases specifically addressed to them. These writings were at least accesible at all times. Consequently, any undue stressing of the baptizing of dying infidel infants would have added fuel to the fire of persecution already rampant. Even in modern times, the Congregation of the Propaganda has cautioned missionaries concerning the use of discretion and secrecy in the matter, and the omission of Baptism in cases where it is otherwise licit, but may bring persecution or hatred of Christians.[2]

In the fifth century, when Christianity was already favored by the state, evidences can be found which are indicative of the general attitude, which are quite general in their statements, and which can cover all cases. A local council of Carthage (401) commends the *legati Maurorum fratres nostri,* because they redeem many barbarians whom they have baptized.[3] This redemption is obviously to prevent perversion in the future. In fact, the practice seems to have grown to such proportions that Pope Leo I (444-461) found occasion to

2 E. g., S. C. Prop. F., April 17, 1777, ad 1, Coll., no. 522.
3 c. 111, D. IV, *de consec.*

rebuke those whose indiscrete zeal led them to baptize hostages who fell back into paganism on return to their own country.[4] The same Pope ordered the Baptism of foundlings and children recaptured from the enemy, after enquiry had been made as regards any previous Baptism.[5] Local abuses existed in Spain in the sixth and seventh centuries,[6] which also appear in a local council of Paris (614).[7] Jews were compelled to be baptized, probably due to the interference of the civil power in Spain, where the councils were composed of representatives of both the Church and the state. The eighth ecumenical council, Nice II (787) contains a canon which seems to be specifically directed against such local practices.[8]

In the eighth and ninth centuries there does not seem to be more explicit testimony. Canons of local synods and the collections of the statutes of St. Boniface contain regulations worded in general terms, but do not with certainty indicate the practice in the case of dying infants of non-Catholic parents. Thus, St. Boniface orders the conditonal Baptism, after investigation, of children baptized by heretics, priests are to carry the holy oils and chrism with them on journeys for cases of necessity, and any priest is to baptize a sick child brought to him,[9] etc.

2. *The Decretum and Mediaeval Theologians.*

Much of the past legislation, already cited, is found in the *Decretum Gratiani*, e.g., the canon of Carthage, and the questions answered by Pope Leo I, but no new

4 c. 111, D. IV, *de consec.;* for fuller text, Cavallera, *Thesaurus*, no. 1040.

5 c. 113, D. IV, *de consec.;* for fuller text, Cavallera, *Thesaurus*, no. 1041.

6 c. 14, Toledo III (589), Hef.-Lecq., III, p. 227; c. 60, 61, 63, Toledo IV (633), Hef.-Lecq., III, p. 274-275. Cfr. Council of Toledo, 652, 680, 693, 694.

7 c. 4, Paris (614), Hef.-Lecq., III, p. 929.

8 c. 8, Hef.-Lecq., III, p. 782.

9 cs. 4, 18, 32, 31, Hef.-Lecq., III, p. 929-932.

development appears.[10]

In the schools, however, the question of the *right* of the Church, without much current information as to the fact or practice, becomes the subject of discussion. Durandus denied the validity of Baptism conferred on infants of Jews and infidels against the wishes of their parents.[11] St. Thomas, whilst maintaining the validity of such Baptisms, answers without distinction that they are illicit, and violate the natural right of the parents.[12] Scotus held that a prince could laudibly command it, but must take care that such parents do not kill the children.[13] There is no theoretical difficulty concerning the children of heretical parents.

3. *Modern Times.*

The mediaeval theologians had not considered specifically the case of *dying* infants of non-Catholic parents. With increased missionary activities, this question became extremely practical. In Christian countries, except in regard to Jews, it had not been very practical, as heretics baptized validly in most instances. In the responses gathered in the Collectanea (1622-1906) permission to baptize the dying infants of all non-Catholics is always conceded.[14]

(a). *The Dying Infants of Infidel Parents.*

A response of the Holy Office, January 28, 1637,[15] helped to settle the matter practically. Then, the alternative is given, either *articulum mortis,* or the removal of the infant from the power of the parent, etc.[16] But some doubt remained concerning the theory and the practice in regard to the infants of Jews. Hence, Pope

10 cs. 111-113, D. IV, *de consec.*
11 In 4, D. IV, q. 7, a. 13.
12 *Summa* III, p. 68, a. 10; II-II, q. 10, a. 12.
13 Sent. 4, D. IV, q. 9, a. 2.
14 E. g., S. C. S. Officii, January 28, 1637, Coll., no. 90.
15 Instr. S. C. de Prop. F., April 17, 1777, VI, Coll., no. 522, which cites several earlier responses, and calls attention to the need of caution to avoid hatred; S. C. S. Officii, July 22, 1840, Coll., no. 902.
16 E. g., S. C. S. Officii, August 24, 1703, Coll., no. 259.

Benedict XIV in his letter *Postremo mense,* February 28, 1747,[17] expounded the theory particularly in reference to the infants of Jewish parents, and settled the practical applications. In case of danger of death, or abandonment by the parents, the baptizing of such infants is laudable.

The only difficulty that now remained was in regard to the danger of death required. This does not mean *periculum commune et vagans,*[18] but in the same instruction the attention of the missionaries is called to the fact that sickness, plague, etc., are far more likely to prove fatal in uncivilized than civilized regions. It also lays down a general principle: "Doctorum opiniones ad Ecclesiae decreta sunt exigendae, non ipsa decreta ad opinantium libitum inflectenda."[19] In the nineteenth century, the decisions use the term *periculum* and not *articulus mortis.*[20] Moreover, the wording seems to be more binding. Finally, *periculum* is distinguished from *articulus mortis,* Baptism is declared licit in both cases, and the very expression of the Code is also used in the third question:

1. An possint baptizari filii infidelium in periculo, non vero in articulo mortis constituti.
2. An iidem possint saltem baptizari, quando non est spes eos denuo revisendi.
3. Quid si valde prudenter dubitetur, *quod ex infirmitate, qua actu afficiuntur,* non vivant, sed moriantur ante aetatem discretionis?

R. Ad 1, 2 et 3, Affirmative.[21]

---

17 *Opera,* XVI, vol. 2, p. 170-191, cfr. no. 8, p. 172, no. 9, p. 173-174.

18 Instr. S. C. de Prop. F., April 17, 1777, VII et VIII, Coll., no. 522: ". . . quidquid interdum velut per synonymam vocem nomine articuli mortis exprimitur, non autem loquuntur de illo communi et vaganti periculo, in quod nec vocabulum nec notio articuli mortis ullo modo convenit."

19 Ibid., VI .

20 E. g., S. C. S. Off., July 22, 1840, Coll., no. 902; S. C. S. Off., December 11, 1850, ad 6, Coll., no. 1054.

21 S. C. S. Off., July 18, 1894, Coll., no. 1877.

(b). *The Dying Infants of Heretical Parents.*

There never was any doubt concerning the *right* of the Church to baptize the infants of baptized persons. A decision, however, specifically stated that the Church certainly has the right, but the *cardo difficultatis* is that she "exequi non potest, *nec periculum amovere* . . ."[22] In cases in which such parents offer their infants for Baptism, administration of Baptism is licit:

> Instante vero mortis periculo, aut quolibet valetudinis vitio infecti praedicti parvuli, quo prudenter decessuri credantur antequam annos discretionis attingant, non modo licet, sed sollicite curare debent missionarii . . . tunc enim cessat proximum perversionis periculum, atque aeternae saluti infantis necessario remedio citra culpam, imo etiam cum merito ministri, prospicitur.[23]

This is for a case in which the parents are willing to have their infant baptized. The same Instruction applies the general principles where the parents are unwilling: "in extrema necessitate, in qua quilibet alius baptizari potest."[24]

(c). *The Infants of Mixed Marriages.*

There is no particular danger of death required that such infants may be baptized. The Church regards the existence of one Catholic parent as sufficient ground in even normal cases for the elimination of the danger of perversion,[24b] also when the infidel party

---

22 S. C. S. Off., January 21, 1767, Coll., no. 465.

23 Ibid., cfr. Litt. Ap. *Postremo mense*, Benedicti PP. XIV, February 28, 1747, Coll., no. 360, for infants of infidels, under similar circumstances.

24 Coll., no. 465.

24B E.g., S. C. S. Officii, February 8, Coll., no. 9, and in footnote; S. C. S. Off., October 12, 1600; S. C. S. Off., November 29, 1672, Coll., no. 205 (one party heretic); Const. Bened. PP. XIV, February 2, 1744, ad 6, Coll., no. 345 (father a Turk); S. C. S. Off., November 18, 1745, Coll., no. 353 (a rather full response covering the principles and cases which may arise); S. C. S. Off., July 6-8, 1898, ad. 4, Coll., no. 2007.

is unwilling,[25] and the infant will *later* be baptized again by a non-Catholic minister.[26] If the Catholic party were an apostate, the infant under normal circumstances may be baptized on her offering it and after her absolution.[27] Another interesting case was solved, in which two parties, one a Catholic, the other a Jew, were civily married: the Catholic party is *in articulo mortis.* The response is that if there is a *spes possibilis* of the future Catholic instruction, the infant may be baptized; otherwise, only *in mortis articulo.*[28]

C. The Present Law.

1. *Licit Baptism.*

An infant of infidel parents can be licitly baptized, even though the parents are unwilling, *cum in eo versatur vitae discrimine, ut prudenter praevideatur moriturus, antequam usus rationis attingat.*[29] The same holds *generatim* for the infants of two baptized non-Catholics.[30]

2. *Possibility of Fulfilling Conditions for Normal administration.*

The clause, *etiam invitis parentibus,* is employed, so that both the father and the mother, and *a fortiori* those who take their place, may be certainly opposed, and with the full knowledge of this fact by the minister. But in the hypothesis that the conditions contained in canon 750, par. 2, for the administration of Baptism to such infants outside of the danger of death are possible of fulfillment in such danger, is there an *obligation* of securing them? The canon in question is giving the rule for cases in which the parents are will-

25 Cfr. preceding footnote, especially coll., no. 345.
26 S. C. S. Off., November 29, 1672 (heretic), Coll., no. 205; S. C. S. Off., September 19, 1765 (schismatic), Coll., no. 460.
27 S. C. S. Off., February 8, 1624, Coll., no. 9.
28 S. C. S. Off., July 6, 1898, Coll., no. 2007.
29 Canon 750, no. 1.
30 Canon 751.

ing or unwilling *etiam invitis parentibus*. Past responses of the Holy See have ordered the secret Baptism, and see a certain danger to the common good of Catholics, as already stated, in imprudent zeal.[31] However, as there is question of moral probability in regard to the foreseen death before the use of reason, prudence would suggest that where the conditions of the second section can be easily secured, they should be obtained.[32]

3. *The Only Conditions Required.*

The simple terms, *articulus* or *periculum mortis,* oftentimes used in the past, do not appear. This may be due to the fact that the former term might be given too restricted a signification, and the latter too extensive a meaning. Thus, in canonical and theological usage, the term *periculum mortis* is capable of stretching over many years; *articulus mortis,* on the other hand, might give rise to unnecessary scruples. In the case of Baptism, the line of demarkation between *infans* and *adultus* is fundamentally the use of reason and not the age. Further, danger of perversion arises with the use of reason. Hence, a limit is placed to the *discrimen vitae.* Two conditions are really implied: first, a *periculum mortis;* and, secondly, a prudent judgment that death will come before the use of reason.

It naturally follows that the *discrimen* must be personal to the infant, and actually here and now present in the degree required. The wording of the canon demands this,[33] the old law confirms it,[34] and the can-

---

31 E. g., Instr. S. C. de Prop. F., April 17, 1777, ad 1, Coll., no. 522.

32 Canon 750, no. 2, gives the conditions in question:

No. 2. Extra mortis periculum, dummodo catholicae eius educationi cautum sit, licite baptizatur:

1. Si parentes vel tutores, aut saltem unus eorum, consentiant;

2. Si parentes, idest pater, mater, avus, avia, vel tutores desint, aut ius in eum amiserint, vel illud exercere nullo pacto queant.

33 Canon 750, no. 1: ". . . cum in eo versatur vitae discrimine, ut prudenter praevideatur moriturus, antequam usum rationis attingat."

34 Lehmkuhl, *Theo. Mor.*, II, no. 84; Cfr. S. C. S. Off., July 18, 1894,

onists are agreed.[35] The actual death need not take place until some time before the use of reason, but this must be morally certain at the time of the Baptism. The canon does not use the term *articulus mortis,* nor is it necessarily demanded, e.g., an infant with some disease, which in the prudent judgment of the one to administer Baptism satisfies the condition, is a fit subject for immediate Baptism, even though the actual death will not take place before the use of reason. However, as has already been explained, if the child, although less than seven, has actually the use of reason, it falls under the canon governing the Baptism of adults when dying.

In the particular case, the intensity of the *discrimen* can be determined in accord with past responses of the Holy See, by local conditions, medical advancement, etc.[36] The existence of an indeterminate or common epidemic in a locality, as, for example, a plague, will not give ground for the Baptism of *all* the children, unless it is affecting the lives of each of the infants actually in the degree required.[37]

4. *Does the Code Impose an Obligation?*

At various times, the Holy See has called the attention of missionaries to the possibilities of baptizing dying infants of non-Catholics, ordering that they follow the decrees of the Holy See in this matter rather than private opinion.[38] The Instruction vehemently exhorted the missionaries to leave no stone unturned in securing the Baptism of such infants.[39] The present canon uses the terms *licite bapitzatur.* But there is

---

ad 3, Coll., no. 1877; Instr. S. C. Prop. F., April 17, 1777, ad VII et VIII, Coll., no. 522.

35 Vermeesch-Creusen, II, no. 33, 2; Blat, *Com. T. J. C.,* III, p. 40.

36 Instr. S. C. Prop. F., September 8, 1869, ad 46, Coll., no. 1346.

37 Instr. S. C. Prop. F., April 17, 1777, Coll., no. 522; cfr. Vermeersch-Creusen, II, no. 33.

38 Instr. S. C. Prop. F., April 17, 1777, ad VI, Coll., no. 522.

39 Ibid., ad VI, VII, VIII; cfr. Instr. S. C. S. Off., January 21, 1767, Coll., no. 465.

need of prudence and expediency in view of the avoidance of greater public evils, even granted that the condition required is certainly present. The fear of persecution and hatred are greatly lessened in modern times in some pagan countries, for example, in China and Japan, by the inroads made by western ideas, and particularly in the former country by the revolution and the consequent removal to a large extent of the main barriers, custom and tradition. But even in these countries this can hardly be said with equal truth in regard to all regions. In other countries, due to the domination of Christian powers, for example, in India, the fear is almost negligible. Add to these facts the increasing number of missionaries, the favorable attitude of the infidels, and perhaps greater application can be made of these canons.

5. *Infants of Mixed Marriages.*

Where one of the parents is a Catholic, the condition required for dying infants of two infidels, heretics, etc., does not apply. The general rule is that they are to be baptized in the same manner as infants of Catholic parents, as long as the Catholic party is living.[40] The Church has a right to baptize these infants, and in view of the past legislation, already cited, it would appear that the existence of the Catholic party, apart from real apostasy on his part, provides a *spes possibilis* that perversion will be averted in some way. If the Catholic party is dead, and the infant is in the control of the non-Catholic party, obviously the ordinary rule in regard to a dying non-Catholic infant must be applied.[41]

D. The Fundamental Principle.

The Angelic Doctor, without distinction, considered

40 Cfr. canons 756, no. 3, 1061, no. 1, 1, 1071, 2316.

41 S. C. S. Off., July 6, 1898, Coll., no. 2007; cfr. S. C. S. Off., October 12, 1600, Col., no. 9 (footnote); S. C. S. Off., November 18, 1745, Coll., no. 353.

that the Baptism of the infants of infidels, against the wishes of their parents, was a violation of the natural right of the parents: "Si vero nondum habent usum liberi arbitrii, secundum jus naturale sunt sub cura parentum, quamdiu ipsi sibi providere non possunt . . . et ideo contra justitiam naturalem esset, si tales pueri invitis parentibus baptizarentur."[42] He also urges that it would be dangerous to baptize such *propter naturalem affectum ad parentes.* Pope Benedict XIV stated that it was necessary to introduce a distinction, teaching that it was laudable to baptize such infants, against the wishes of their parents, when they were dying.[43]

Some modern theologians maintain that the natural right of the parents is to the company of the child, and that the administration of Baptism when the infant is dying does not interfere with this right.[44]

All rights and duties in this world, as all human activity, are merely means to man's ultimate end. Thus, nature vests the rights of the infant in the parent, but only in so far as the parents do not exercise this power to militate against the infant's salvation. But in the case of an infant who will die before the attainment of the use of reason, the only possible means by which it can attain a supernatural end is Baptism. Hence, if the parents are unwilling to permit the Baptism of their infant in such a case, no right of theirs is violated in the administration of Baptism.

The second reason—the danger of perversion—urged by St. Thomas, in the humble opinion of the writer, seems to be the fundamental principle in the present canons. Thus, in canon 751, which concerns

42 *Summa,* III, q. 68, a. 10 (*Respondeo*).
43 *Postremo mense, Opera,* XVI, p. 170-191.
44 Pesch, *Prae. Theo. Dogm.,* VI, no. 455-462.

baptized persons, there can be no question of violation of rights. In fact, a past response of the Holy See expressly stated that the danger of perversion was the *cardo difficultatis*.[45] But the same restrictions are placed as in Canon 750. This is likewise true of the infants of two apostates. It is also obvious from the constant responses of the Roman Congregations already cited. Three things can efficaciously remove the danger of perversion: physical death before the attainment of the use of reason; the future Catholic education of the infant; and, finally, permanent mental death, i.e., habitual insanity from infancy. In all three cases, the Code permits Baptism.

It would not be excessive to state that the Church has in the abstract the right to baptize all infants, which she exercises in the case of all habitually insane from infancy, checked only by expediency. But this in application is for the individual welfare, which must yield to the public good, whenever it seriously menaces it. Thus, the exercise of the Church's full rights in the matter would undoubtedly bring disruption of the peace and harmony among races and nations, hatred and persecution to the members of the Church. Past responses, already noted, cautioned against imprudence under these heads. Further, St. Thomas, whose reason is incorporated in responses of the Holy See,[46] urges that where the use of reason is morally certain, perversion is likewise morally certain. Hence, St. Thomas cites the examples of saints chiding Christian emperors for commanding the Baptism of the infants of their infidel subjects.[47] The Angelic Doctor also calls this the constant custom of the Church,

45 S. C. S. Off., January 21, 1767, Coll., no. 465.

46 Cfr., e. g., Litt. Ap., *Postremo mense*, Benedicti PP. XIV, February 28, 1747, Opera, XVI, p. 170-191. St. Thomas, *Summa*, III, q. 68, a. 10.

47 *Summa*, II-II, q. 10, a. 12. Cfr. Instr. S. C. de Prop. F., April 17, 1777, ad VII et VIII, Coll., no. 522.

which Pope Benedict XIV admits. But Benedict XIV himself in his constitution *Postremo mense* stated that a distinction had to be introduced in the view of St. Thomas between dying and healthy infants.

2. *Baptism of Abnormal Adults.*

The danger of culpable and effective perversion is greatly lessened by the general weakened condition of the mental powers of abnormal adults. If the insanity is from infancy and habitual, the subject is in the same mental condition as an *infans.* But the degree of abnormality, relative to Baptism, must be judged on the basis of whether the subject is capable of committing a morally imputable grave sin or not. If the person never had this amount of reason, he is *habitualiter amens,* but this state must have begun before the attainment of the use of reason, and last until death. If, however, at any period of his life, he had, or at present has, or is likely to obtain this use of reason, the canons regarding *infantes* cannot be applied. Such conditions are facts, and thus must be proved and not presumed. They are not entirely adults, nor *infantes,* but midway between these two classes. Hence, the Code contains a special canon concerning them, as follows:

> 1. Amentes et furiosi ne baptizentur, nisi tales a nativitate vel ante adeptum rationis usum fuerint; et tunc baptizandi sunt ut infantes.
> 2. Si autem dilucida intervalla, dum mentis compotes sunt, baptizentur, si velint.
> 3. Baptizentur quoque, imminente periculo mortis, si, antequam insanirent, suscipiendi baptismi desiderium ostenderint.
> 4. Qui lethargo aut phrenesi laborat, vigilans tantum et volens baptizetur; at si periculum mortis impendeat, servetur praescriptum par. 3.[48]

48 Canon 754.

1. *Rare Cases.*

An Instruction of the Propaganda, April 17, 1777, gives much practical guidance in rare cases. It directly concerns *amentes* and children of four or five years, who either certainly or doubtfully perceive the principal mysteries of faith. The ultimate test, already cited, is that they know the difference between good and evil, and be capable of sinning.

(a). It can be morally certain that the persons in question have such a faculty, in which case the rule of St. Thomas is applied, namely, they are adults in reference to Baptism.

(b). It can be morally certain that they do not enjoy such a faculty, in which case distinctions have to be introduced: either (i) it is prudently judged to be a perpetual lack of the amount of reason in question, and then the subject is always an *infans;* or (ii) there is hope of the faculty coming in the future, in which case a further distinction is introduced: either (a) the subject is in danger of death, and can be baptized without scandal, the doubt being solved in favor of the Christian religion and faith, and the spiritual salvation of the one to be baptized, i.e., Baptism is to be administered; or (b) there is no danger of death, in which case more certain signs of reason are to be awaited.

(c). The matter can remain wholly doubtful and uncertain, in which case, if necessity does not urge, the minister can and must wait for more suitable and greater knowledge; but if necessity urges, then in case of doubt, "inclinandum in favorem religionis et fidei christianae, et spiritualis salutis baptizandi."

The same Instruction also declares that it is shameful negligence to disregard such persons, but caution must be used in the avoidance of danger to the public good of Catholics.[49]

49 Ad II, Coll., no. 522. (The substance of this important Instruction is given in the text.)

2. *Habitually Insane.*

No restrictions are placed in the case of the habitually insane; they can always be licitly baptized, with or without the *discrimen* required in the case of infants of infidels.

3. *Those with Lucid Intervals and Insane* AFTER *the Use of Reason.*

Those who had or have lucid intervals, or became insane after the use of reason, are to be baptized if they wish it, while they are of sound mind. The only condition demanded, when they are in danger of death, is that *baptismi desiderium ostenderint.* It is obvious, however, that the third section of the canon is concerned only with those who are actually insane at the moment of death, *antequam insanirent.* The second section of the same canon covers the case of those who have lucid intervals, but at the time of the ministration of the priest are *sui compos.* The second section only expressly refers to the intention of Baptism, but in harmony with canon 752, and many past responses of the Holy See, the conditions in that canon will have to be satisfied in so far as possible. This will be treated in greater detail under the following section. Extreme caution, however, is necessary, due to the weakened mental condition of the subject, the circumstances, and the danger of lapsing into insanity in bad faith.

The case of those who are insane when they are dying is more difficult. Obviously in this hypothesis, present signs will have little rational meaning, hence the third section of the canon, unlike the third section of canon 752, refers not to a past or present sign, but "si, *antequam* insanirent, suscipiendi baptismi *desiderium ostenerint.*" But whereas canon 752, par. 3, demands "vel antea vel in praesenti statu *manifestaverit* aliquo *probabili* modo *intentionem* illum suscipiendi,'' canon 754, par. 3, is satisfied with a desire. A desire is less in the psychological order than an intention, as the former is the beginning of the act of the will, whereas the latter is its completion. The reason of this distinction probably can be found in the effects of insanity, which weakens the whole mental equipment, especially the will. But the will is the seat of both intention and rational desire. Hence, much less positive formal proof seems to be required in the case of the abnormal for the fulfillment of the canon. If even this minimum of evidence cannot be obtained, the grounds for applying the general presumption in the second chapter regarding intention seem to be extremely slight. Insanity is mental death, but is not preceded by the same mental attitude as physical death, that is, the circumstances preceding the latter, such as the close approach of eternity, and dread of punishment, love of God, etc., are presumed to give rise to an act of at least attrition, but these are all absent in the case of the former. One rarely knows that insanity is coming nor believes the verdict of the best doctors, but death is more certain and awe-inspiring. Some authorities, however, permit conditional Baptism even in this case.[49]

4. *Coma and Delirium.*

High fevers are usually accompanied, even in the case of those who have been normal all their lives, by a period of temporary mental derangement. Coma is equivalent to unconsciousness, and may endure until the actual death of the subject in some diseases. *Delirium tremens,* and suchlike conditions, would seem likewise to fall under the fourth section of the present canon. The ordinary rule is that such persons can be baptized, only on the suspension of these conditions,

49 Vermeersch-Creusen, II, no. 36; Genicot, *Inst. Theo. Mor.*, II, no. 150.

sufficiently at least to permit of advertence and the expression of an intention. Obviously, canon 752 will have to be satisfied to the fullest extent possible under the circumstances. If, however, they are in danger of death, the only condition with which this discussion is concerned, the third section of the present canon will find application. But in regard to the general presumption in chapter two, there is a difference. Psychologists and physicians teach that very often in a subject in the state of coma, consciousness may be present internally, which it is impossible to manifest externally. In the case of delirium in high fevers, a minimum of rationality is possibly present so as to satisfy the general presumption. *Delirium tremens,* however, is caused by such over-indulgence as to exclude the probability of the general presumption in the moment of death, unless there is ground for thinking that sufficient consciousness is present to elicit the acts necessary to satisfy it. However, on the basis of this possibility at the moment of death, and some slight probability of canon 754, par. 3, being satisfied, conditional administration of the Sacraments seems permissible.[50]

3. *Baptism of Dying Normal non-Catholic Adults.*

The canon of the Code reads as follows:

> 1. Adultus, nisi sciens et volens probeque instructus, ne baptizetur; insuper admonendus ut de peccatis suis doleat.
> 2. In mortis autem periculo, si nequeat in praecipuis fidei mysteriis diligentius instrui, satis est, ad baptismum conferendum, ut aliquo modo ostendat se eisdem assentire serioque promittat se christianae religionis mandata servaturum.
> 3. Quod si baptismum ne petere quidem queat, sed

50 Cfr. Vermeersch-Creusen, II, no. 36, 5, 37.

vel antea vel in praesenti statu manifestaverit aliquo probabili modo intentionem illum suscipiendi, baptizandus est sub conditione; si deinde convaluerit et dubium de valore baptismi collati permaneat, sub conditione baptismus rursus conferatur.[51]

A. Historical Survey.

1. *Introduction.*

It would seem that until comparatively recent times legislation which expressly deals with dying non-Catholics concerns only those who in some manner formally converted to the Catholic religion, or at most those who have given some sign of their intention. The testimonies touch those who are destitute of their senses, and give some sign, hardly the third class, who gave no sign. But, on the other hand, this is likewise true of the present Code. Theologians have taught and continue to teach today that the general presumption as outlined in the second chapter permits of the possible administration of the Sacrament of Baptism to such.

2. *Sacred Scripture and the Apostolic Fathers.*

Our Lord gave a general command to His Church, "Going therefore, teach all nations, baptizing them."[52] The mission is not to baptize all men, but to teach first and then baptize those that believe.[53] Thus, St. Peter instructed Cornelius,[54] Philip the Samaritans[55] and the eunuch,[56] and, in fact, St. Luke's Gospel is said by

51 Canon 754.

52 Mt., XXVIII, 19.

53 Mt., XXVIII, 19; Mk. XVI, 16; Cfr. John VI, 66 (divine call); Roms. X, 17; I Tim. II, IV; St. Augustine, *De gratia et libero arbitrio* 14, 29 (R. de J., no. 1940); *De correptione et gratia* 7, 12 (R. de J., no. 1946); *Contra Julianum* 4, 8, 44 (R. de J., no. 1906).

54 Acts X, 33, 34-37. Cfr. instruction before baptizing after the descent of the Holy Ghost, Acts II, 14-35, but they had to do penance first, 38, but were baptized on that day, 41.

55 Acts VIII, 5-6, 12-13.

56 Acts VIII, 36-38. The instruction was very short, but the request is express.

some to be the first written catechism for Theophilus.[57] In many cases contained in Sacred Scripture, the instruction was quite short.[58] A profession of faith and renunciation of evil is expressly mentioned in Sacred Scripture,[59] and certainly implicitly contained in many passages.[60]

St. Justin Martyr requires persuasion and belief,[61] conviction and assent,[62] profession of faith and renunciation of evil [63] for Baptism. The Pastor Hermas tells of those who wish to be baptized, but are unchaste, and so draw back.[64]

Thus far, no specific testimony can be adduced to cover the case of dying non-Catholics. But the elements demanded for the licit administration of Baptism are clear, with a possibility of contracting these in extraordinary cases and necessity.

3. *The Post-Apostolic Fathers.*

Tertullian considered hasty reception of Baptism irreverent,[65] and in common with St. Clement of Alexandria [66] demanded a penitential period of preparation.[67] The profession of faith and renunciation of evil are still further emphasized.[67] Tertullian distin-

---

57 Luke I, 3-4: "It seemed good to me also . . . to write to thee in order . . . that thou mayest know the verity of those words in which thou hast been instructed." Thus, it would seem that the Gospel was intended for the further instruction of Theophilus after Baptism.

58 E. g., v. a., Acts XVI, 18 (Lydia); I Cor., II, 1, 4, 6; III, 1, 2; Acts IX, 18 (Baptism of St. Paul).

59 Acts VIII, 31 (the eunuch); XXII, 16 (St. Paul); XVIII, 8 (Philippian jailer); XIX, 5 (no mention of request).

60 I Cor., 1, 12-16, etc.

61 *Apol.* 61; R. de J., no. 126.

62 *Apol.* 65; R. de J., no. 128.

63 *Apol.* 61.

64 Bk. II, Vis. III, 8; MPG, 2, 906-908.

65 *De Bapt.*, 20; MPL, 1, 1222-1224.

66 *Strom.*, 6, 15; MPG, 9, 339-353.

67 *De Bapt.* 20, 1-4; Kirch, no. 198.

67 St. Irenaeus, *Adv. Haer.* 3, 12, 8; MPG, 7, 902 Tertullian, *De Bapt.* 6; MPL, 1, 1206; *De Idol.* 8; MPL, 1, 639-640; *De Corona* 3; R. de J., no. 367; *De Spect.* 4; MPL, 1, 635-636; Hippolytus, *Phil.* IX, 10; ANF, V, p. 132-133; (the last testimony is quite detailed, but the work is of doubtful authorship).

guished solemn and private Baptism, directing the former to be given only at Easter and Pentecost,[68] but permitting the latter to be administered in necessity even by the laity.[69] St. Clement of Alexandria gave the reason for demanding intention "for God compels not" as it is repugnant and derogatory to Him to do so.[70] But in the view of Tertullian, intention and reverence for the Sacrament are so overemphasized as to lead him to refuse Baptism to infants.[71]

There is a growing tendency, probably due to the influence of Marcion, whereby certain classes are excluded from Baptism, but even he is willing to admit them on their deathbed.[72] The most interesting testimony of this period is in the complaint of Hippolytus that Pope Callistus admitted even "lascivious and wicked," "if only any of them be a believer."[73] This writer was a violent adversary of the Pope, so that interpreted in an orthodox sense, it probably means that the Pope was willing that no one should be excluded from Baptism, merely because he had been a very grave sinner in the past.

4. *The Councils.*

The council of Elvira (305) excludes no willing unbaptized person, although for some it reserves Baptism until they are dying, e.g., *flamines,* those troubled with evil spirits, a *meretrix,* a catechumen guilty of adultery and abortion.[74] This council permits any *fidelis* to administer Baptism in necessity, but excludes an apostate, which represents a compromise with the schismatics.[75] The council of Arles (314) is willing to

68 *De Bapt.* 20; MPL, 1, 1222-1224.

69 *De Bapt.* 17; Kirch, no. 197.

70 *Quis dives salvetur?* 10; MPG, 9, 614.

71 *De Bapt.* 18, 10-14; Kirch, no. 197.

72 Tertullian, *Contra Marcion* 4, 11; MPL, 2, 380-383.

73 *Refut.* 9, 7; MPG, 17, 3386. Cfr. Tertullian, *De Pudicitia* 1, MPL, 2, 980.

74 Cfr., 11, 37, 39, 42, 44, 69, 38, Hef.-Lecq., I, 221.

75 c. 38.

admit all who *credere volunt.*[76] The first ecumenical council of Nice I (325) raises no objection to these canons, although it expressly cites a canon of the council of Arles in at least one instance. It seems, then, that the practice of not denying Baptism to any person who was dying and wishing to receive it, even though they had been public sinners, was already well established.

The subsequent local councils and writers discuss the *kind of manifestation* of consent required, and other incidental questions. In a council of Hippo (393), it is enacted that if relatives testify for the desire of those sick and unable to speak any longer, they are to be baptized,[78] which was repeated in Carthage IV (397). Although not necessarily representing very extensive practice, it is found in the *Decretum Gratiani* (1140-1150): "Egrotantes, si pro se respondere non possunt, cum voluntatis eorum testimonium sui dixerint, *baptizentur.* Similiter et de penitentibus agendum est."[79] This testimony is truly remarkable. Canons of the council of Orange (441) enact, one becoming suddenly dumb may be baptized if he indicates his wish by signs, while there is no mention of any sign in the case of those possessed, and to those who have lost their reason "all the blessings of religion shall be granted."[80] The council of Laodicea (343-381) regulates cases in which very little instruction was given as these dying persons on recovery shall be made to learn the *Creed* by heart, and to understand the gift bestowed on them.[81]

4. *Conclusions Regarding This Early Period.*

Sufficient testimony has been adduced to indicate

76 c. 6, Hef.-Lecq., I, 280.

77 c. 13; Hef.-T., I, p. 420; c. 128, D. IV, *de consec.*

78 Hoppi, c. 32, Hef.-T., I, p. 407-8; Mansi, III, 851; Carthage, IV, c. 75, for Penance, orders the giving of the Holy Eucharist on this.

79 c. 75, D. IV, *de consec.*

80 cs. 1, 3, 12, 13, 14, 13, 40; Hef.-T., III, p. 160-162.

81 c. 47; Hef.-T., II, p. 321.

the spirit of the Church. While it is true that much of it is oriented by local details, there remains sufficient evidence for the statement of the attitude on essentials. In the case of any kind of dying non-Catholic, irrespective of the past, evidence of the desire alone, even through others, sufficed in extreme cases. Local abuses, referred to in an earlier section, did exist in Spain and in Paris, but the principle that no one can be compelled to receive Baptism is clearly stated in the case of Jews in the ecumenical council, Nice II (787). St. Augustine stated a principle, which strictly speaking, seems to refer to catechumens, who passed into unconsciousness without giving any very definite signs: "Catechumenis ergo in huius vitae ultimo constitutis, seu morbo seu casu aliquo si compressi sint, ut quamvis adhuc vivant, petere sibi tamen baptismum vel ad interrogata respondere non possint, prosit iis quod eorum in fide christiana iam nota voluntas est, ut eo modo baptizentur, quo modo baptizantur infantes. Non tamen propterea damnare debemus eos, qui timidius agunt quam nobis videtur agi oportere . . . Baptizare non audent eos, qui pro se respondere nequiverint, ne forte contrarium gerant voluntatis arbitrium. . . . Sed non solum incredible est nec in fine vitae huius baptizari catechumenum velle, verum etiam, *si voluntas eius incerta est, multo satius est nolenti dare quam volenti negare, ubi velit an nolit sic non apparet,* ut tamen credibilius sit eum, si posset, velle se potius fuisse dicturum ea sacramenta percipere, sine quibus iam credidit non se oportere de corpore exire."[82]

6. The Corpus Juris.

The *Corpus Juris* contains a summary of the past.[83] The subject is expected first to accept the *rudimentum*

82 *De adult. conjug.* 1, 26, 33; R. de J., no. 1862.
83 c. 74, 75, 77, D. IV, *de consec.*

fidei,[84] elsewhere identified with the learning of the *symbolum fidei.*[85] He is, however, not to be driven to Baptism by sharp words, and violence is not to be used on the Jews.[86] Only *parvuli* are exempt from the requirement of penitence for past sins.[87] The intention of the subject is absolutely required for validity, but in this connection the words of Pope Innocent III are cited, which have given rise to much controversy.[88] This desire, however, can be manifested through others.[89]

7. *Modern Times.*

The spread of missionary activity gave renewed occasion for the application of the practices of the past. In pagan lands, many difficulties arose in regard to the amount of instruction, intensity of sorrow, purpose of amendment, and especially the nature of the intention and its manifestation.

B. The Present Law.

I. *Cases of Formal Conversion.*

Canon 752, par. 1 and par. 2, states the general law for cases of dying non-Catholics, who formally convert in some manner. The danger of death is not in itself a sufficient reason for reducing the usual requirements for the licit and valid administration of Baptism on an adult. The Code, in the first paragraph of the canon cited, states a general rule, which obliges (*ne baptizetur*), if morally possible, to the degree in

84 c. 54, D. IV, *de consec.*

85 cs. 58, 59, D. IV, *de consec.*

86 cs. 93, 94, D. IV, *de consec.;* cfr. cap. 9, X, *De Judaeis, Saracenis, et eorum servis,* V, 6.

87 c. 95, 96, 97, D. IV, *de consec.* An abstinence of forty days is imposed on Jews before Baptism, c. 98, but penitence is not absolutely necessary for Baptism, c. 99, Ibid.

88 c. 3, X, *De Baptismo et eius effectu,* III, 42. Pope Benedict XIV in the *postremo mense* refutes cajetan's use of this passage to establish his opinion concerning a neutral intention (*Opera* Tom. XVI, p. 185, *Postremo mense,* February 28, 1747, nos. 48, 49).

89 c. 75, D. IV, *de consec.*

which it is morally possible, and must be observed, even in the case of the dying.[90] But added to this physical condition of danger of death are usually other aggravating circumstances, e.g., proximity of death itself, considerably lessened keenness of mental capacity in the grasping of spiritual realities and truths, even a diminished facility in the eliciting of volitional acts, etc. In a word, suffering or general lowered mentality, and external interferences grow with the dying condition to moral and eventually physical impossibilities. The Church in her canons makes due allowances for all these circumstances.

1. *Normal Requisites.*

An adult is not to be baptized, unless he is knowing and willing, and properly instructed; in addition he must be warned to be sorry for his sins.[91] The term "adult" is understood in the sense already explained.[92] The reception of Baptism is in the case of an adult a most solemn and important rebirth into Christian society, and not a mere external rite. Hence, it demands all the requirements for a full rational act. This involves full knowledge and advertence as regards the act itself. Full consent of the will must also be present, as it is not an external mark of internal beliefs. But the act of the will, which in itself is a blind faculty, demands knowledge of the content of the obligation undertaken, both in regard to belief and moral precepts to be observed. The will only acts rationally to the extent that it is motivated by the intellect. The reception of Baptism marks the incorporation of the subject into the most perfect society given to men, which carries with it obligations in respect to the past and the future life. No actual sin is

90 Genicot, *Inst. Theo. Mor.*, II, no. 149-150.
91 Canon 752, no. 1.
92 Cfr. chapter II, no. 1.

forgiven without some kind of sorrow, nor is a new life seriously embraced without due resolution being made to live up to its mandates for the future. Hence, at least attrition for past actual sins and a resolution in respect to the future will also be required.

2. *Moral Impossibility.*

(a). *Danger of death.*—The person must be in danger of death, from any cause whatsoever, that there be a lessening in the usual requirements. But this circumstance will not suffice in itself, as the Code also demands that fuller instruction be given, unless it be morally impossible.[93]

(b). *Intention.*—An express desire of receiving Baptism is demanded for the certain validity of Baptism.[94] If possible, this must be positively and externally stated in unmistakable terms. The Church also requires for the liceity but not the validity of the Sacrament, that the subject be advertent and attentive to what is taking place. There is some concession even on these points in responses of the Holy See. The intention must contain some positive elements, in these circumstances, although it may remain, due to moral impossibility, doubtful in content.[95] If possible, this intention must be actual, but if this is morally impossible, it is sufficient for licit administration that it be "if not actual, at least virtual, and interpretative, as the theologians call it . . ."[96] A *purely* superstitious or temporal intention is not sufficient while there is time to instruct, but in case

93 Canon 752, no. 2: ". . . si *nequeat* in praecipuis fidei mysteriis diligentius instrui" . . .

94 Cfr. Instr. S. C. S. Off., August 3, 1860, Coll., no. 1198, which contains a summary of the conditions required; S. C. S. Off., May 10, 1703, Coll., no. 256. Cfr. also, Lehmkuhl, *Theo. Mor.*, II, no. 77; Cappello, *De Sacrs.*, I, no. 155, 85.

95 Add to preceding, S. C. S. Off., April 10, 1861, Coll., no. 1213; S. C. S. Off., March 30, 1898, Coll., no. 1993; S. C. S. Off., September 18, 1850, Coll., no. 1050.

96 Instr. S. C. S. de Prop. Fide, May 8, 1779, Coll., no. 534.

there is not, no official response exists which prevents action on such an intention, in the face of impossibility of securing more definite information.[97] It will not be sufficient for valid Baptism, if the *purely* superstitious intention is the principal one, and there is a positive exclusion of the right intention. But if further information cannot be obtained, some intention, although doubtful, is present, and Baptism must be administered conditionally. Where there is doubt about the existence or nature of the intention, or the fact or validity of a possible previous Baptism, the conditional form must be used.[98]

(c). *Instruction.*—There is a distinct concession in the canon itself in regard to the fulness of instruction necessary. If it is morally impossible to give a more diligent instruction in the principal mysteries of the faith, it is sufficient, in danger of death, that the subject show in some way he assents to them. The more diligent instruction in the mysteries can be omitted, but not some little instruction, as some knowledge of them is required, so that the subject *ostendat se eisdem assentire.* The words *praecipuis fidei mysteriis* seem to mean something more than those necessary, certainly or probably, by necessity of means. In past responses of the Holy See concerning Baptism, two phrases are found, *praecipua* and *mysteria necessariae necessitate medii.*[99] In one response,

97 S. C. S. Off., March 8, 1776, Coll., no. 477; but cfr. Const. Alex. VII, January 18, 1658, XV, Coll., no. 129.

98 Cfr. canon 752, no. 3, and 732, no. 2.

99 E. g., in a response of S. C. S. Off., March 8, 1770, Coll., no. 477, the missionary is warned to instruct an adult in the rudiments of the Faith, even if he is old, which is to be repeated on recovery. In the response, S. C. S. Off., January 25, 1703, ad 2, Coll., no. 254, explanation of "mysteria fidei quae sunt necessaria necessitate medii, ut sunt *praecipue* mysteria Trinitatis et Incarnationis" was demanded. The term "principal mysteries" is used in an Instruction S. C. de Prop. de Fide, May 8, 1779, Coll., no. 534, and S. C. S. Off., May 12, 1830, Coll., no. 813. Finally, an Instruction has *according to the capacity of the individual,* Instr. S. C. Off., August 3, 1860, Coll., no. 1198, but in doubt Baptism is to be conferred; cfr. also S. C. S. Off., April 10, ad 1, 1861, Coll., no. 1213.

the former includes explicit belief in Our Lord and the positive moral precepts of the divine law,[100] but the general signification seems to involve instruction according to the mental capacity of the subject, in so far as is morally possible under the circumstances.[101] Controverted points, which do not involve an error on the fundamental truths, which are likely to *change* the good faith of the subject into bad, can be avoided. Thus, in the case of dying Masons, a previous response conceded, where further instruction or demands would not be productive of good results, and the dying man is *bona fide,* it is sufficient that he be exhorted to assent in a *general way* to the mandates of the Church.[102] Again, in an exceptional case, where there was danger of turning the good faith of a dying savage, previously instructed by Calvinists, into bad, the reading of the Apostles' Creed in his presence with his assent to it sufficed, as far as the instruction is concerned.[103] But it is quite clear that rational assent to truths understood according to the mental capacity and not mere affirmation to please the minister, etc., is required.[104] The promise of receiving instruction in the future will not in itself suffice, except where the person is wholly *incapax,* but in the extreme case instruction in the bare essentials will suffice, e.g., the mysteries of the Blessed

---

100 S. C. S. Off., May 10, 1703, ad 2 et 3, Coll., no. 256.

101 Even in case of catechumens in good health, the missionary need only enter into those details, which prudence permits, S. C. de Prop. Fide, September 12, 1645, XIII, Coll., no. 114. In the response S. C. S. Off., May 10, ad 1, 1703, Coll., no. 256, concerning the dying as well, the adult must understand and believe *iuxta proprii captus mensuram.*

102 S. C. S. Off., July 8, 1874, Coll., no. 1419: ". . . sufficere quod in genere hortentur ut se sincere subiiciant ecclesiae auctoritati, atque mandatis S. Sedis, deinde *baptizari atque absolvi* possint." Cfr. Reuter-Lehmkuhl-Umberg, *Neo-Confessarius,* nos. 203, 218.

103 S. C. S. Off., January 27, 1892, Coll., no. 1780; cfr. S. C. S. Off., April 10, 1861, ad 1, Coll., no. 1213: ". . . dummodo iisdem fidei mysteriis vel simplici oris affirmatione, vel nutibus saltem, ostendant se consensum praebere."

104 S. C. S. Off., May 10, 1703, Coll., no. 256.

Trinity, the Incarnation, and the Redemption.[105] The obligation of fuller instruction on recovery remains.[106] Since the Creed seems to contain the principal mysteries, as distinguished from those necessary by necessity of means for salvation, the canon would be satisfied by assent to it with some explanation. If possible, it would seem that enough should be imparted to the dying person to give him at least a confused notion of Christianity in general, and more or less definite ideas on the truths necessary by necessity of means. This will depend on circumstances and the mental capacity of the individual.

(d). *Assent.*—It is sufficient that the dying person show in some manner that he assents to them. In human affairs, especially in the case of the dying, such assent can be made by simple affirmation in words which indicate that one accepts what is presented, or by equivalent signs, e.g., a nod, sigh, etc. In a word, anything that in some way shows that he accepts the truths presented will suffice. A hearing of what is said, without necessarily grasping intellectually more than the fundamentals, is sufficient.

(e). *Promise for the future.*—A serious promise is required in regard to the mandates of the Church, and their future observance. This promise again involves a knowledge, at least in essentials, on the general principle, *Nihil volitum, quin praecognitum.* It is, however, principally concerned with the future rather than the past. The knowledge can be very general and confused, in accordance with the circumstances. But the Church does not wish the immaculate law of Christ

105 S. C. Off., January 25, 1703, ad 2, Coll., no. 254: "Non sufficere promissionem. . . ."

106 S. C. S. Off., March 8, 1770, Coll., no. 477: ". . . et si senes tardiores memoria fuerint, iteratis instructionibus eorum succurrant imbecillitati." In the case of deaf-mutes who are in danger of death: "Curent . . . autem missionarii eo meliori modo quo possunt, ut eos postea mysteria saltem principilia edoceant, . . ." S. C. S. Off., December 11, 1850, ad 1, Coll., no. 1054.

to be confounded with idolatry or gentile institutions, which are out of conformity with the natural law.[107] Idolatry will have to be absolutely removed, because it is in conflict with the fundamental truths necessary for salvation. Polygamy and similar practices will also have to be given up.[108] But if the danger of death is proximate, provided the subject is in good faith, and bad faith will probably follow, past responses seem to give ground for omission of specific warning in these matters.[109] If one is living in a necessary occasion of sin, which is beyond the power of the subject to remove, in proximate danger of death, he may be baptized. A special disposition of mind was required in a case of girls *desponsatae* to infidels or polygamists, which illustrates this point. Baptism can be conferred in danger of death: ". . . ob peculiares circumstantias gravesque causas . . . omnino requiritur talis eius animi dispositio, ut, si dispensari nequeat, potius mori velit, quam sacrilegum irritumque matrimonium contrahere."[110] Thus, in danger of death, the *intention* will suffice, which finds expression in a serious promise.

II. *Cases in Which the Intention Is Manifested in Some Probable Manner.*

Canon 752, par. 3, states the general law for such cases.

1. *The Physical State of the Subject.*

The second section of the present canon considered cases in which the subject is in danger of death, but

107 Const. Alex. PP. VII, January 18, 1658, XIV, Coll., no. 129.

108 Instr. S. C. de Prop. F., October 18, 1883, XVII, Coll., no. 1606 (for normal cases). Cfr. S. C. S. Off., January 29, 1805, Coll., 680, which contains the case of a man who had sold his wife and illegitimately taken another: Baptism is permitted in grave infirmity, "privatus non maneat medio ad aeternam salutem tam necessario." The Instr. S. C. S. Off., March 28, 1860, Coll., no. 1188, takes up the matter in detail, which concludes, "sive polygamus, sive concubinae omnino a statu fornicationis recedere debunt. . . ."

109 Instr. S. C. S. Off., June 20, 1866, Coll., no. 1293, polygamists in the hour of death, if disposed.

110 Instr. S. C. S. Off., June 20, 1866, III, Coll., no. 1293.

with whom the minister can communicate. The third embraces cases in which the subject is dying, but cannot communicate with the minister in any certain manner, "if he cannot even seek Baptism. . . ." The distinguishing factor is not *periculum mortis,* which is obviously presupposed, but the physical impossibility of certain communication between the minister and the subject. This may be due to causes primarily arising from the state of the subject or the minister. Thus, destitution of the senses on the part of the subject will satisfy the conditon.[111] Examples of such cases on the part of the minister are also given in past responses of the Holy See, e.g., deaf mutes may be baptized by a minister who is totally ignorant of the sign language, if they give *aliqua signa religionis,* or are unable to make any definite sign, a minister may baptize a person of whose language he is totally ignorant.[112]

2. *The Intention.*

The canon uses the terms *intentionem illum susci-*

---

111 S. C. S. Off., March 30, 1898, ad 3 Coll., no. 1993. The parallel with canon 752, no. 3, is very striking:

1898 and 1850.	Canon 752, no. 3.
"Si antea dederint *signa* velle baptizari, vel in praesenti statu aut nutu aut alio modo eamden dispositionem ostenderint, *baptizari posse sub conditione,* quatenus tamen missionarius, cunctis rerum adiunctis inspectis, ita prudenter iudicaverit."	"Quod si baptismum ne petere quidem queat, sed vel antea vel in praesenti statu manifestaverit *aliquo probabili modo* intentionem illum suscipiendi, *baptizandus est sub conditione;* si deinde convaluerit et dubium de valore baptismi collati permaneat, sub conditione baptismus rursus conferatur."

The differences are worthy of note:

1. In the 1898 response a distinction is introduced between the evidence from the past (signa), and the present (alio modo); in canon 752, no. 3, the evidence from the past and the present are placed on the same footing (aliquo modo probabili);

2. In the 1898 the *possibility* of baptizing conditionally was conceded to the missionary, and the final judgment in the matter left to his prudent judgment; in canon 752, no. 3, an obligation is imposed.

The 1898 response concerned the case of one who was a Mohammedan, which also is very significant.

112 S. C. S. Off., September 18, 1850, Col., no. 1050 (Ignorance of language). S. C. S. Off., December 11, 1850, ad 1, Coll., no. 1054 (Deaf-mutes).

piendi. . . . Hence, any kind of intention suffices, with only one qualification as to its content, namely, that it be an intention of receiving Baptism. Speculations on the possible content of such an intention, manifested *aliquo modo probabili,* are not considered by the canon. Provided that the man furnishes the requisite evidence of receiving the Sacrament of Baptism, he must be baptized conditionally. Under the circumstances there is a lack of actual knowledge in regard to the content or form of the intention, which only the actual facts and no amount of theological speculation will supply. Theories on the kind of intention required will find place *si deinde convaluerit.* The danger of forcing Christianity on the dying man is taken care of by the manifestation of some kind of intention.

The minister need know nothing concerning the religious faith of the dying subject. If there is the required amount of evidence concerning the intention, i.e., its existence, not its content, the canon imposes an *obligation* of baptizing him conditionally. This is quite clear from a comparison of the present canons and past responses.[111] Thus, an adult Mohammedan, who became destitute of his senses *nihil prorsus ei dicendo . . . baptizari posse sub conditione,* if somewhat similar conditions to those contained in the third paragraph of the present canon are satisfied. But a final clause was added that this should be done, if, considering the circumstances, the missionary *ita prudenter judicaverit.*[112] This evidently was the established norm, as an older decree of the Holy Office, concerning negroes, placed under similar circumstances, is cited.[113] The present canon uses clauses which differ slightly from the responses. But there is a great difference from viewpoint of obligation *baptizandus*

113 S. C. S. Off., September 18, 1850, Coll., no. 1050. Cfr., S. C. S. Off., March 20, 1686, Coll., no. 230, ad 8.

sub conditione replacing *baptizari posse sub conditione* and the final clauses. There is no question of past life or creed, or future possibilities in the canon, but the existence of the *intentio illum suscipiendi* alone. The Baptism must be conditional, as due to the possible vagueness of the manifestation *aliquo modo probabili,* the Sacrament is of doubtful validity. As long as this condition of the subject continues, further enquiry will not throw much light on the validity of the Baptism conferred. So the canon prescribes that the enquiry *de valore baptismi collati* shall be made on the recovery of the senses or later.

3. *What Is a Sign?*

The response of 1898 used the term *signum* in reference to the evidences drawn from the dying man's past life, and for the present condition phrases capable of a much wider interpretation *aut nutu aut alio modo. . . .* The canon applies the final phrase to both the past and the present, but inserts the word *probabili,* i.e., *aliquo modo probabili,* and possibly somewhat further limits this by the use of the verb *manifestaverit.* In human affairs, an express and precise statement is by no means demanded for the manifestation of an intention, as it can be implicitly contained in some other action. Past responses provide examples relative to Baptism. Thus, it can be "*aut nutu aut alio modo,*" which the missionary "*cunctis rerum adiunctis inspectis ita prudenter iudicaverit.*"[111] In the case of deaf mutes with whom the missionary is unable to communicate, it is "qui dant aliqua religionis signa. . . ."[114] Or, in a pagan country, the rejection of idolatry of one's free will.[115] Membership in a Christian sect that

114 S. C. S. Off., December 11, 1850, ad 1, Coll., no. 1054.

115 Ibid., ad 2. In the question two conditions were stated; first, that they had rejected idolatry; and secondly, that they were not enemies of Christianity. In the response, the only condition mentioned is "in proximo et moraliter certo articulo mortis, et quod antecedenter abrenuntiaverint idololatriae."

does not totally and absolutely reject the Sacrament of Baptism ought to create a presumption concerning the existence of an at least implicit intention. The question of its definite content, and sufficiency for validity can only be investigated in the actual case with a knowledge of the facts from the subject himself.

III. *Cases in Which There Is Absence of Knowledge Which Cannot Be Supplied.*

At the outset, the writer does not wish to invoke any greater certainty for the application of an at least extrinsically probable opinion in this particular section than was established in the second chapter.

Cases may confront the minister in which he is left in the dark in regard to the intention of the subject. If he knew the dying person in the past, this lack of knowledge will not be so absolute. If some of the friends of the dying man are at the bedside, much information can be obtained from them, with the use of prudence. In such instances, however, probably the *aliquo probabili modo* of canon 752, par. 3, can be satisfied.

If none of these factors will help in solving the difficulty, the case is altogether extraordinary, and possibly no rule can be stated. In the abstract, there is a possibility of administering the Sacrament conditionally, but extreme prudence and caution are necessary. Experts assert oftentimes persons, who are apparently dead and cannot communicate with those around them, understand what is taking place. Hence, in the hypothesis that they are opposed to the reception of Baptism, its administration may easily turn their presumed good faith into bad. The methods and means of avoiding this must be left from their very nature to the prudence of the minister.

Theologians and canonists extend the possibilities of administering conditional Baptism beyond that of the canon, which states the obligation—the law—without reprehending the possibility of more extended action.[116] Some authors point out that no response clearly determined the limits of possible action, or condemned more extensive views.[117] They were well known and taught before the Code, and so have lost none of their force since its appearance. The question was in regard to the obligation and not the probability of this opinion, among the pre-Code supporters of the view.[118] The Code is silent in the matter. The logical conclusion, then, is that the probability of the opinion remains, although there does not seem to be an obligation of following it, and the whole matter is left to the prudence and tried zeal of the individual minister.

In general, then, this difficult matter must be left, until greater certainty is had concerning the considerations outlined in the second chapter.

IV. *What Is to Be Done in Case of Recovery?*

The Code states in Canon 752, par. 3: ". . . si deinde convaluerit et dubium de valore baptismi collati permaneat, sub conditione baptismus rursus conferatur," which must be taken in conjunction with Canon 732, par. 2: "Si vero prudens dubium exsistat num revera vel num valide collata fuerint, sub conditione iterum conferantur."

If the sick man recovers, the validity of the Sacrament, not its fruitful reception, is the subject of investigation. If he had a positive intention to the contrary, then it has to be conferred absolutely, provided the conditions required for this are fulfilled. In judging this intention, however, the opinions of theologians

116 Lehmkuhl, *Theo. Mor.*, II, no. 78; Vermeersch-Creusen, II, no. 35; Genicot, *Inst. Theo. Mor.*, II, no. 450; Cappello, De Sacrs., I, no. 159; Pesch, *Prae Theo. Dogm.*, VI, no. 439 (who chides Suarez in this matter, but places the reservations already noted).

117 E. g., Lehmkuhl, l. c.; Genicot, l. c.

118 E. g., Lehmkuhl, l. c.; it would seem that Lehmkuhl himself believed in the existence of an obligation.

must be taken into consideration, so that if the dying man had sufficient intention to satisfy any opinion that has extrinsic support which renders it the basis of a *prudens dubium,* the conditional and not the absolute form must be used. Obviously, where the first or second paragraph of canon 752 are possible of application, doubt that would effect the validity must be removed before the Baptism is conferred. Only where the third section of this canon, or the possible extension, which has been outlined, are applied should there ordinarily be room for a prudent doubt concerning the validity. A positive intention is required by many theologians for *certain* validity, and this must be the basis of the minister's judgment after the recovery.

The words of Pope Benedict XIV can well conclude this section: "Fieri enim potest (nec casus sane hic metaphysicus est) ut ipso in actu intentionem habuerit sufficientem, diabolicis deinde stimulis incitatus, et victus, ad vomitum rediturus mendacium proferat, et de intentione interrogatus nigrum pro albo, ut inquiunt, repraesentet."[119]

---

119 *Postremo mense,* February 28, 1747, no. 50, cfr. 51, which seems to have some bearing on the question, *Opera,* XVI, p. 186. "51. Quod si nulla sit reliqua dubitatio, planeque constet hac luce clarius, adulto Baptismum accipienti nullam prorsus fuisse voluntatem, aut intentionem, nil restat aliud, quam eumden et hortari, et admonere, ut rite id faciat, quod jam irrito fecit, et suscipiat absolute, ac libere Sacramentum; ac si obstinate repugnet, tum nihil aliud superest, nisi ut remittatur. Si autem res in dubio sit, nec intelligi possit, an defuerit intentio, an sufficiens adfuerit necne, adultus tum retinendus, baptizandusque *sub conditione:* S. Thomas 3, par., q. 68, art. 7. . . ."

CHAPTER IV.

PENANCE AND DYING NON-CATHOLICS.

1. Possibility of Administering the Sacraments.

The Code contains a general norm, which embraces the ministration of the Sacraments to all classes of baptized non-Catholics:

> Vetitum est Sacramenta Ecclesiae ministrare haereticis aut schismaticis, etiam bona fide errantibus eaque petentibus, nisi prius, erroribus reiectis, Ecclesiae reconciliati fuerint.[1]

The exclusion of Sacramental communication of heretics and schismatics is very ancient. Heresy involved positive error and contamination of the doctrine of Christ.[2] It placed groups and individuals outside of the Church. Consequently, communication with them in such sacred relations as the administration of the Sacraments demanded was naturally regarded by the early Fathers and Christians as treachery to Our Lord. Schism, on the other hand, did not at first place its members completely outside of the Church. But the test of orthodoxy was externally manifested in sacramentally communicating with those alone who were in full accord with the apostolically founded churches.

1. *The Dogmatic Basis of the Canon.*

The divine law clearly forbids *communicatio in di-*

1 Canon 731, no. 2.

2 Mt. XVIII, 17-18: "And if he will not hear the church, let him be to thee as the heathen and the publican." The *Didache,* IX, 5 (R. de J., no. 6), states: "Nemo autem edat neque bibat a vestra eucharistia, nisi qui baptizati sunt in nomine Domini; de hoc etenim dixit Dominus: Ne date sanctum canibus." St. Ignatius, *Ad. Phil.* IV (R. de J., no. 56); "Studeatis igitur una eucharistia uti. . . . ."; *Ad Smy.* VII, 1 (R. de J., no. 64); "Ab eucharistia et oratione abstinent, eo quod non confitentur eucharistiam carnem esse Salvatoris nostri Jesu Christi. . . ." Etc. Cfr. cs. 49, 131, 143, D. IV, *de consec.*

vinis with all who are not fully in accord with the visible Church.[3] The reception of Baptism, it is true, makes one a subject of the Church, but full membership in the Church as a visible society demands much more. For the Church is the congregation of all the faithful, who profess the same faith, participate in the same Sacraments and Sacrifice, and are subject to their lawful pastors, under the one visible head, the Pope. Any baptized person, not observing all of these conditions, although a subject of the Church, is in a state of defection or rebellion. Now, the chief social bonds whereby the Church visible unites her members to herself and her spouse, Christ, are the Sacraments. The Church has never declared that validly ordained ministers, even though outside of her visible membership, administer invalid Sacraments, but clearly asserted the contrary principle against the Novatians and Donatists. Nor does she deny that those in good faith, even though outside of her visible fold, receive the Sacraments from these ministers validly and licitly. But both heretics and schimatics, even though invisibly within the Church, are externally and publicly outside of it. Hence, she must in virtue of the divine command, gravely prohibit her ministers communicating sacramentally with all in a public *state* of rebellion, culpably or inculpably.

The Catholic Church absolutely condemns the Branch Theory. She, in virtue of her divine foundation, is the sole visible mystical body of Christ on earth. All other branches, even though they have validly ordained ministers who administer valid Sacraments, are completely severed from the sole and only tree of Christ. But the Sacraments are placed absolutely in the hands of this one true Church of

3 Cfr. Mt. XVII, 17-18; Lk. X, 16; Mt. X, 40; Mt. VII, 6.

Christ. She must guard zealously, protect, and defend them against irreverence. All sacramental grace, however, flows from Christ to men through her hands alone. But the Sacraments give grace *ex opere operato non ponentibus obicem.*[4] The only absolute obex for the reception of the Sacraments of the dead is a positive will to the contrary, and the lack of the conditions on the part of the subject required for validity. In the case of the Sacraments of the living, ordinarily this obex will be the absence of grace in the soul. But even a recipient, who is a heretic or schismatic, may provide the conditions required for the valid and formally licit reception of the Sacraments, as far as he is concerned. Hence, although the administration of the Sacraments to such is gravely illicit, the reception of them by him is neither formally nor sinfully illicit nor invalid on his part. In which case, the recipients receive the grace through the one true Church, and not any branch. In a word, the condition or state of the minister, apart from lack of the required intention or jurisdiction, does not prevent him from acting, validly although ordinarily illicitly, as a minister of the Catholic Church.[5]

4 Council of Trent, Sess. VII, *De Sacrs. in genere*, can. 6, 8. Cfr. Tanquerey, *Syn. Theo. Dogm.*, III, nos. 300-306, footnote p. 214. Pesch, *Prae. Theo. Dogm.*, VI, nos. 312-313; nos. 109-130: "Obex invenitur in solis adultis et est *defectus voluntatis*, fidei, paenitentiae, non vero quaelibet ineptitudo recipiendi Sacramentum, sicut baptizatus non est aptus, ut iterum baptizetur. * * *"

5 Cfr. Hurter, *Theo. Dogm.*, III, no. 337, who states that it is *de fide* for Baptism (Council of Trent, Sess. VII, *De Baptismo*, can. 4), and *fidei proximum* for the other Sacraments, with the exception of Penance, on account of jurisdiction, which the Church supplies in the case of the dying. Pesch, *Prae. Theo. Dogm.*, VI, nos. 241-245, advances as the theological argument that the minister of the Sacrament is the instrument of Christ. A validly ordained priest, even though heretical or schismatical, can administer the Sacrament of Penance *in articulo mortis;* "Imo valet etiam de sacerdote haeretico vel schismatico, sed in solo casu necessitatis licet cum talibus communionem in sacris habere," Ibid., VII, no. 425. St. Alphonsus, no. 560, 1, accepts the negative opinion as more probable even *in articulo mortis*, but changed his mind of this question later, Quaest. reform., 19 (VI, no. 560, footnote

The Church must strictly prohibit her ministers from licitly administering the Sacraments until the public bond is restored between the recipient and her external communion. This will be absolute for Sacraments of the external forum, which demand a public *state* of union with the visible membership of the Church. In the case of Sacraments of the internal forum with extreme spiritual necessity and physical impossibility of external union, this demand is not so absolute, as will appear in the further development of this discussion. As the defection is a public state, it follows that the reunion must be of the same nature, if morally possible. Hence, even in the extreme cases, where externalization is physically impossible, the Church permits her minister to act, only on the presumption that this reconciliation has been effected internally in the last moments of the dying person.

This legislation of the Church is neither unduly severe nor unnatural. As the one and only true Church founded by Christ, she must demand that all her members be in union with her. But one who has been in a public state of rebellion or disunion, even inculpably, can do his share in the restoration of the public bond by rejecting his error and professing belief in the doctrine of the Church. Moreover, as a society, the Church has a right to demand this fulfillment of certain conditions before she will readmit rebellious subjects. Thus, the children of one who has become the naturalized citizen of another country have no rights in the father's original mother-country. If they wish to regain what he has abandoned, a new oath of allegiance and an elaborate process are demanded. Only after these have been gone through will the original

6). Cfr. Vermeersch-Creusen, III, no. 468, 6; Tanquerey, *Syn. Dogm. Theo.*, III, no. 399; Noldin, *De Sacrs.*, III, no. 43 (however, only in so far as the ministrations *in articulo mortis* are concerned).

mother-country renew formal social national bonds with him. In a higher and more perfect manner, this is true of the Church. She is a divinely founded society, and as such must observe the laws given by her Founder.

2. *The Nature of the Obligation.*

The canon states a positive law, flowing from the divine command of her Founder.[6] It imposes a very grave obligation on the minister and the recipient. In itself, however, it does not affect the validity of the Sacraments. This is dogmatically defined in the case of Baptism.[7] Holy Orders administered by validly ordained schismatics and heretics, granting that the other conditions required for validity are present, are also valid. The Church clearly taught this against the Novatians and the Donatists.[8] The same is also true of the Sacraments of Confirmation and the Holy Eucharist. Thus the Holy See has allowed only the conditional repetition of Confirmation conferred by a schismatic, when it is probably invalid for some other reason.[9] There is no response of the Holy See which declared their ministrations of Penance to the dying invalid. Today, it is quite clear in the Code that all priests validly absolve all penitents, otherwise fulfill-

6 Cfr. notes (2) and (3) to this chapter. Also Mauritio de la Taille, *Mysterium Fidei* (Parisiis, 1921), p. 387-388.

7 Coun. Trid., Sess. VII, *De Baptismo*, can. 4.

8 E. g., Pope Anastasius II (496-498), Denz., no. 169; Pope Gregory I (590-604), Denz., no. 249; Clement VIII (1592-1605), Denz., no. 1087; Code, c. 951. Cfr. c. 1 (from the general council, Latern III), 2 (Innocent III), X, *de schismaticis et ordinatis ab eis*, V, 8. Anglican Orders were pronounced invalid because of defect of form and intention, *Apostolicae curae*, September 13, 1896.

9 E. g., the response of the S. C. S. Off., July 5, 1853, Coll., no. 1095, distinguished, and acquiesced in the Confirmations administered by these *priests* in places where the faculty was not expressly revoked in Valachia, Moldavia, and Asia. In a letter of the Holy Office, March 16, 1872, repetition in cases in which Confirmation had been administered by schismatical *priests* was not judged expedient, unless Tonsure or Orders were to be received, or the parents requested it. Then it was to be conditional and secret. It would seem that a *penicillium*, used by some Orientals, played a prominent part in later decisions.

ing the other conditions required for validity, in danger of death.[10] The phrase used by the present canon, *Vetitum est,* clearly does not pertain to validity. From viewpoint of the penitent, if he provides the conditions required for the valid reception of the Sacraments, there is no reason why he should not receive them validly. The Catholic doctrine is that the Sacraments give grace *ex opere operato, non ponentibus obicem.* Hence, if he is unaware of his obligations of renouncing error, which he does not recognize as error, and professing the full faith of Christ, of which he is unaware, there is no reason why he should not receive the grace of the Sacrament. He will then be fulfilling this obligation materially and to the best of his ability. But the obligation is very grave on the part of the minister. He must warn even a dying person, and secure the abjuration and profession, in so far as possible.

(The nature of the abjuration and profession, which satisfies this canon in the case of the dying, will be discussed later in the chapter.)

3. *The Typical Cases.*

In a discussion of the intention required for the licit and valid administration of the Sacrament of Penance to dying heretics and schismatics, three cases have to be carefully distinguished; first, those in which there is some kind of formal conversion on the deathbed; secondly, those in which there is some probable manifestation of this intention, and the desire of receiving Penance; and, thirdly, those who gave and can give no sign.

2. Historical Survey of the Relations of the Church to Dying Heretics and Schsmatics.

1. *Introduction.*

The Church in her public relations with heretics and

10 Canon 882.

schismatics must repudiate them. Some of them may be in invisible communion with her, but public law concerns the external and not the internal state. Under the extraordinary circumstances of approaching death, even public law concedes much modification in the fulfilment of its demands. The extreme case, however, is not a matter for public law, but prudence and action in the spirit of the law. The Church is ever zealous in the avoidance of scandal to her subjects, and consequently is not likely to make a matter of public law what may cause laxity or harm. If it is true today that the Church leaves much to the prudence of her ministers, it is much more true of the earlier days of her history.

There are early testimonies that cover the cases of some form of conversion in danger of death, and those in which signs have been given by the subject or others. It is quite certain that the Sacraments were refused to no dying person who sought them in any way, but nothing definite can be stated as to how this had to be done. In comparatively recent times, responses can be cited which permit action on the supposition that implicit reconciliation has taken place in the dying moments. In the early ages, usually the ministers were validly ordained, even though heretics or schimatics, so that dying persons could well be left oftentimes to their ministrations. Today, very few of the heretical sects have validly ordained ministers, unlike their schismatical brethren, so that the problem has changed in nature. Another change is worthy of note in regard to the belief in the Sacrament of Penance. Most of the schismatics believe in it as Catholics do, and so can be considered to have an intention of receiving it in their dying moments. This is not usually the case with Protestants, with the exception of High Church Anglicans. Hence, as long as they are conscious, in addition to reconciliation, some specific instruction on Penance is required. But withal bigotry against the Catholic religion is fast on the decline, and a more open mind seems to prevail generally, of which the fast increasing number of converts is an evidence. But to return to the history, in the early ages, heretics and schismatics had regularly validly ordained ministers, who could satisfy the needs of their dying brethren. Even today they have this power under the Code.[12] Hence, there was no special need for legislation, except in cases in which some kind of conversion took place, or signs of reconciliation were manifested. In modern times, very few heretical ministers, as they are not validly ordained, can be the channel of this jurisdiction, even in the case of the dying.[13]

2. *The Apostolic and Post-Apostolic Fathers.*

The condemnation of heresy and schism are manifest in the Sacred Scriptures.[14] The implicit divine prohibition of ministering to them sacramentally also finds place.[15] But more precisely the texts concerning the "irremissible sin" or the so-called "unforgiveable sin" provided food and tissue for the rigorism of the first five centuries.

The Apostles themselves recognized heresy as a very grave sin.[16] The Apostolic Fathers adopted the same view, but distinguished it from schism. Repentance is possible in the case of both sins, but is much easier in the case of schism.[17] The Post-Apostolic

12 Canon 882. Cfr. cs. 2261, 2284.

13 Anglican orders were declared invalid, due to lack of intention and form. Apostolicae curae, September 13, 1896. Cfr. Pesch, *Prae. Theo. Dogm.*, VI, nos. 226-227: a validly ordained heretical or schismatical bishop can confer valid Orders, Ibid., nos. 660, 664.

14 Cfr. chapter I, no. 1.

15 Cfr. notes to this chapter, (2) and (3).

16 Cfr. chapter I, no. 1.

17 The *Didache* contains a general warning: "Ne derelinquas mandata Domini; custodies vero quae acceptisti, neque addens neque demens" (IV, 13; R de J., no. 2). It also urges to create *episcopi,* and

Fathers drew a distinction between the fierce and the mild, the leaders and the simple.[18] Repentance is very difficult for the former, but again much easier for the latter. The difficulty of repentance, however, is based, not on the impossibility of the Church receiving them back, but on their own pride and bad will, and the nature of error, which prevent them from repenting. This sin of heresy is also recognized as having very bad effects on the community in general. Hence, in the restoration of the guilty, the personal perversion needed remedial regeneration, and the spiritual injury and scandal to the community at large called for some process that would deter others and purge out the cancerous effects of this spiritual disease. In an attempt to prevent these evils, and those of other gross sins, the system of public penance naturally developed. In our humble opinion, it represents medicinal mercy

warns: "Ne igitur contemnatis eos" (XV, 1-2; R. de J., no. 10). Pope Clement wrote his Epistle to the Corinthians precisely that the condition of *schisma* might be brought to an end (*I Cor.* LVII, 1; R. de J., no. 27). St. Ignatius warns against those who: ". . . habentes perversam doctrinam; quos non permisistis seminare inter vos" (*Ad Eph.* IX, 1; R. de J., no. 40), but "familiarum perturbatores regnum Dei non hereditabunt. . . . Talis, inquinatus factus, in ignem inexstinguibilem ibit; similiter et qui audit ipsum" (*Ad Eph.* XVI, 1, 2; R. de J., no. 41). Again, St. Ignatius warns against Judaizers and "ne incidatis in hamos inanis doctrinae . . ." (*Ad Magn.* IX, X, XI; R. de J., nos. 45-47). The dual test is "ut sine episcope nihil egistis . . ." (*Ad Trall.* II, 2; R. de J., no. 48; III, 1; R. de J., no. 49-50; *Phil.* III, 2; R. de J., no. 56): "Ne erretis, fratres mei: si quis schisma facientem sectatur, regni divini hereditatem non consequitur; si quis ambulat in aliena doctrina, cum passione non communicat" (III, 3; R. de J., no. 56).

Cfr. Motry, *The Concept of Mortal Sin in Early Christianity*, p. 18-19. St. Ignatius, *Ad Phil.* III, 2 (R. de J., no. 56), contains a general statement calling on all who are out of communion with the bishop to do penance: ". . . quotquot paenitentia ducti redierint ad unitatem ecclesiae. . . ."

18 E. g., St. Irenaeus, *Adv. Haer.* I, 10, 1 (MPG, 7, 552), Ibid., III, 23, 3 (MPG, 7, 962). St. Justin, *Dial.* 35 (MPG, 6, 551), states: "et pro vobis (i. e., Jews) et pro aliis omnibus haminibus, qui nos oderunt (i. e., from context includes heretics), precamur, ut nobiscum respiscentes. . . ." Hermas, III, Simil., 8, 6 (MPG, 2, 975-978), calls on them to repent. St. Clement of Alexandria gives an elaborate description of the process of reconciliation of heretics, drawing an analogy between them and the different processes of grafting one limb of a tree on to another.

rather than mitigated rigorism. There is a silence in regard to the treatment of the dying which finds its best interpretation in the light of subsequent testimonies. Reconciliation under ordinary conditions entailed considerable inconveniences, so that, in an age when profession of Christianity meant bitter persecution, any publishing of extreme leniency for the dying would have prevented many making their peace with the Church until then. In a later day, this actually happened in the case of Baptism, which was postponed until the moment of death by some.

In an attempt to interpret the difficult passages of Sacred Scripture concerning the unforgiveable sin, a rigoristic heresy, Montanism, early made its appearance. It taught that the Church has not the power to forgive three sins, among them heresy. Thus, with them the difficulty of repentance on the part of the sinner is changed into an impossibility of remission by the Church. The difference is clear in the case of Tertullian. While orthodox, he holds out the hope of repentance to all sinners, but later joins the Montanists, and excludes the three classes.[19] This heresy was combatted by the orthodox from the very start, and tends to accentuate the mercy of the orthodox teaching, to which Tertullian and his associates take violent exception.[20]

The question of the power of the Church over all sin was thus early asserted. In the meantime, the persecutions grew in ferocity and the Christian community in numbers. A new problem arose, especially in Carthage. Considerable numbers of the Christians yielded to the persecutors, and became apostates either by sacrificing to the pagan gods or obtaining certifi-

19 *De paenitentia* 4 (R. de J., no. 312), cfr. Ibid., 7, 8 (ANF, III, p. 657), orthodox. *De pudicitia* 5 (R. de J., no. 385), heterodox.

20 Cfr. *De pudicitia* (Tertullian), 21 (R. de J., no. 387); Hippolytus, *Phil* IX, 12 (Kirch, nos. 228-233).

cates in testimony that they had done so. St. Cyprian, the Bishop of Carthage, in an attempt to check this, refused reconciliation to them for a time. Again, it is not a question of the power of the keys for him or his party, but of expediency and the due observance of all the formalities and public penances.[21] This is brought out clearly by the fact that in a case in which one of these apostates was over-hastily received by a bishop, he pronounces it valid, but reproves the bishop.[22] The orthodox position in the Lapsi controversy in reference to the dying in particular is quite clear from the order of the Roman Church to St. Cyprian to reconcile all without delay or hesitation, at least when they are in danger of death.[23] The question at stake is not as in the case of the Montanists, the power of the Church, or the sin of heresy as such, but the expediency of public reconciliation, and a particular type of apostasy. It can be concluded with justice that any clemency shown towards these apostates was even truer of heretics. In fact, in these early ages the constant complaint of the unorthodox, such as Tertullian and Hippolytus, is that the Roman Church, under the guidance of the Pope, is too lenient.[24] Wherever there is a question of rigorism, appeal is made to the Pope and the Roman Church, e.g., Firmillian and Novatus appealed to the Pope against the rigorism of St. Cyprian.[25] The testimony of Dionysius of Corinth shows

21 Cfr. D'Ales, *Dict. Apol.*, art. "Bapteme des heretiques," I, p. 411-412, art. "Penitence," nos. 49, 50, and p. 1777. Also chapter IV of this dissertation.

22 *Ep.* 58 (ANF, V, p. 353-354).

23 Cfr. *Ep.* 2, 2, 3 (ANF, V, p. 280-281); *Ep.* 12, 1, 2 (ANF, V, p. 293); *Ep.* 13, 2 (ANF, V, p. 293-294); *Ep.* 14 (ANF, V, p. 294-295); *Ep.* 30, 8 (ANF, V, p. 311); *Ep.* 42 (ANF, V, p. 321); *Ep.* 51, 5, 6 (ANF, V, p. 328-329); *Ep.* 52, 2 (ANF, V, p. 336); *Ep.* 53, 1-3 (ANF, V, p. 336-337). Also add the references in note (21) of this chapter.

24 See notes (19) and (20) of this chapter.

25 E.g., Hippolytus, *Ref.* Bk. IX, 2 (ANF, V, p. 125-126), Noetus went to Rome; Ibid., Bk. IX, 8 (ANF, V, p. 131), Alcibides came to Rome. St. Cyprian, *Ep.* 42 (ANF, V, p. 321), Novatus goes to Rome;

that this leniency was not peculiar to Rome.[26] The struggle between St. Cyprian and Rome also clearly demonstrates that no rigorism would be tolerated by the orthodox.

In conclusion, it may be stated that there is no evidence to show that the orthodox Church, even in these early periods, exercised anything else than extreme charity and clemency towards dying non-Catholics. Its vigorous opposition to all rigorism is positive evidence of this assertion.

3. *Periods of the Councils.*

Montanism, and more particularly Novatianism, were essentially clerical and sacramentalist movements. This rendered both of them all the more serious, particularly in view of the fact that they were regarded as schisms and not heresies by their contemporaries. Moreover, they appealed to the Emperor Constantine, who was more interested in maintaining peace than strict orthodoxy. Hence, these early councils, called at his request, represent attempts at establishing compromises with the schismatics. The members sent the acts of these councils to the Pope for approval, which they did not receive. The council of Elvira (305) prescribes that heretics on returning to the Church are to be granted Penance, but not until after they have done public penance.[27] In the council of Arles (314), held for the same purpose of compro-

---

Ep. 54 (ANF, V, p. 338-347), is a letter to Pope Cornelius against Felicissimus and other heretics, who had appealed; Privatus went to Rome also; St. Cyprian states a general principle in refutation of much interest, "For, as it has been decreed by us—and is equally fair and just—that the case of every one should be heard there where the crime has been committed . . . " (ANF, V, p. 334).

26 Eusebius, *Hist. Eccl.* 4, 23, contains the following: "Dionysius receives back kindly all who have been converted from any falling away, whether of crime or *heretical* depravity."

27 For the calling of these councils by Constantine, cfr. Eusebius, *Hist. Eccl.*, 10, 5, 18-20 (Kirch, nos. 355-356); Ibid., 10, 5, 21-24 (Kirch, nos. 357-358). Elvira, c. 22, Hef.-Lecq., I, 225.

mise, it was decided that those who apostatized from the Church and never either presented themselves for penance or sought it, but seek Communion in an infirmity, "placuit iis non dandam communionem, nisi revaluerint et egerint dignos fructus poenitentiae. . . ."[28] Neither of these councils deny absolution to any dying person, although Arles refuses Communion. The power of the Church is unquestioned, but expediency causes them to put off full external reconciliation until the public penance was done. In this period it would seem that there were two forms of absolution, first, *a culpa,* and later *a poena,* on the completion of the public penance.[29] In the council of Ancyra (314), a modification is introduced, which can be explained on this basis, i.e., apostates must complete the public penance on recovery,[30] and the bishop is given power to reduce or extend it.[31]

The first ecumenical council of Nice I (325) took up and definitely settled the matter. The main difficulty in orthodox circles had been apostasy during persecutions and not heresy, but the council states a general law. The canon is very clear, and extends to all classes of dying persons:

> Regarding those who are passing from life, the *lex antiqua regularisque* shall by no means be deprived of the last and greatly necessary *viaticum* (*ephodiou*). If, after he has been reconciled and has regained communion, he is again numbered among the living, let him have place with those

28 c. 22, Mansi, 2, 469.

29 Pesch, *Prae. Theo. Dogm.,* VII, nos. 30-31, and 41-42; but especially nos. 222-227; no. 225: " . . . in vetere ecclesia tres modi confessionum distinguendi sunt; . . . Ab hoc iudicio utique peccatores condemnabantur ad paenitentiam publicam, sed ii tantum peccatores, qui aut per testes criminum convicti erant, aut ipsi libere confitebantur confessione non sacramentali, sed quae pertinebat ad forum ecclesiasticum."

30 c. 6, Kirch, no. 377. Cfr. cs. 1-5, Kirch, nos. 375-377.

31 c. 5, Kirch, no. 376.

> who have the fellowship of the Prayer only (i.e., the highest class of public penitents). But, generally, in the case of anyone whatsoever who is dying, and who asks to partake of the Eucharist, let the bishop give It to him after due investigation.[32]

Historians of much weight interpret *viaticum* so as to include both Communion and absolution,[33] and even those who do not agree with this view admit that it at least signifies absolution. This *viaticum* is to be given to all when they are dying, and as the second sentence clearly shows, even before it is certain whether they have regained ecclesiastical communion or not, which is reserved until recovery. When one who had been in danger of death recovered, but not until then, if he had been reconciled, public penance was begun in a mitigated form. There is a clear distinction between the conditions for the giving of the *viaticum* and the Holy Eucharist. The former, which certainly includes sacramental absolution from the guilt of sin at least, can be given to anyone who is dying, but the Holy Eucharist can only be administered when the subject has asked for It, and the bishop has decided that he should be permitted to receive It. Thus, in this canon there is a contrast between one who asked and received the permission of the bishop and "those who are passing from life." Evidently, the latter give much less positive grounds for reconciliation than the former. Both the council of Elvira and Arles had required something that resembles signs of conversion. The ecumenical council of Nice, untroubled by schismatics,

32 c. 13, Hef.-Lecq., I, p. 417; Cfr. Watkins, *A History of Penance*, I, p. 291.

33 Cfr. Pesch, op. c., VII, no. 48, 51, who cites many authorities. Hef.-Lecq., I, 417-418, who also cites many authorities, ancient and modern, in proof of the contention that the term includes both Holy Communion and absolution.

with these canons before them, expressly states that a petition is necessary in addition to the permission of the bishop for the reception of the Holy Eucharist by the dying man, but allows the *viaticum* to "those who are passing from life" without any further condition expressed.

The content of this testimony, at least when restricted to sacramental absolution, is undisputed. Some, however, deny that it was a *lex antiqua regularisque*.[34] One thing is certain, the Church sought to root out all rigorism towards the dying from the very start. This canon of the council of Nice is in itself ancient enough to confirm the view that such clemency reigned officially from the beginning, when viewed in the light of evidences already adduced. Subsequent testimonies, which will be cited in the following section, expressly state that whereas Holy Communion was refused to some dying sinners during persecutions for reasons of expediency, Penance *never* was at any time.

4. *Final Settlement of the Question.*

In the fifth century, the denial of absolution is branded as Novatian and reprobated. Thus, Pope Innocent I (405) writes that at no time was Penance ever denied to the dying, although Holy Communion was during times of fierce persecution, lest too great leniency might do harm. After peace was restored, however, Holy Communion was also given, lest the orthodox ("we") seem to follow the bitterness and rigorism of the Novatians. Hence, this Pope orders that *extrema communio* be given with Penance to all dying persons who ask for it.[35] But in some parts Penance, whether private or public is not certain, must have still been denied, as Pope Celestine I (422-432) con-

34 Watkins, op. c., I, p. 291-292. Cfr. Pesch, *Prae. Theo. Dogm.*, VII, nos. 222-227.
35 Denz., no. 95.

demns this practice in very strong terms, and orders *quovis tempore non est deneganda poenitentia postulanti.*[36]

It was required that the dying person ask for penance, whether private or public is not certain, and that forms be observed in regard to public penance and reconciliation. In the council of Nice, the reconciliation was left until the mind of the dying person could be determined, and so the first council of Orange (441) orders that reconciliation of the dying be according to the form of the Fathers with Holy Viaticum *sine reconciliatioris manus impositione.*[37] Thus, there is a clear distinction drawn between the private and the public penance: "If, however, they recover, they must again take their place in the order of penitents, and only after the performance of the proper works of penitence, receive the regular communion (*legitima communio*), together with reconciling laying on of hands."[38] The same council also regulated that the testimony of others or the nod of the dying person can be taken as sufficient sign of the request for penance.[39] Pope Leo I (452) confirmed this practice of taking the testimony of bystanders and expressly included heretics.[40]

Thus, by the fifth century the attitude of the Church is quite clearly defined concerning dying baptized non-Catholics. The heretics thus far did not reject Penance, so that there is no question of their consent to receiving it, or of the necessary intention. At least two testimonies do not expressly demand the request for some form of Penance. In both cases, however, an

---

36 Denz., no. 111. Cfr. Pesch, *Prae. Theo. Dogm.*, VII, no. 57.

37 c. 3 and 4, cfr. Hef.-T., III, p. 160-162, Holy Eucharist refused, says similar to c. 13, Nice I (325) and Carthage IV, c. 76, 78 (398?); Mansi, p. 44; cfr. Carthage IV, cs. 76, 77, 78, Hef. Lecq., I, 416.

38 c. 3, Hef.-T., III, p. 160.

39 c. 12, Hef.-T., III, p. 162.

40 Denz., no. 147, Pope Leo I (440-461).

express request is mentioned in the same testimony as required for the administration of the Holy Eucharist. It would seem that the undertaking of public penance was voluntary, or at least some sign was required on the part of the dying person before it would be imposed. The history is somewhat doubtful in nature, so that a certain conclusion cannot be drawn. The canon of Nice is reaffirmed by subsequent councils,[41] and becomes the guiding principle. In a council of Toledo (680) a strange variation appears; relations of the dying man would take the *votum poenitentiae* for the dying man, which bound him on recovery. The council abolishes this because many on recovery refused to do the penance on the plea that they were totally unaware of what was taking place.[42] This practice reappears with approbation in the statutes of St. Boniface.[43] These evidences would seem to lend additional support to our view, that the sign was absolutely required for the public penance, as here a method is adopted of avoiding this difficulty in cases in which communication with the dying man is impossible. It is worthy of note that the difficulty is in regard to public and not private penance.

5. *Subsequent References to This Period.*

The canons of Nice I, Orange I, and the letters of Popes Innocent I and Celestine I are all found in the *Decretum Gratiani.*[44] In fact, they are the basis of all

41 E. g., Barcelona (540), c. 9; Nantes (658), c. 4; Toledo (675), c. 12; Frankfort (794). c. 37; Statutes of St. Boniface, nos. 18, 31, 32.

42 Toledo XII, c. 2, 8, Hef.-Lecq., III, p. 543-544 (the priest is excommunicated for a year who imposes *public* penance in the absence of clear signs).

43 c. 32, Hef.-Lecq., III, p. 932; cfr. c. 18, Hef.-Lecq., III, p. 931, the last necessary Viaticum must not be refused to any person.

44 c. 4 (a priest is to absolve and Communicate dying persons), 5 (c. 4, Carthage II, if the bishop is absent, a penitent is to be reconciled by a priest in periculo mortis), 6 (an interpretation of c. 12 (Nice I), 7 (Orange 8, c. 3, if dying persons are reconciled without *manus impositione,* they are to be in the rank of public penitents, and receive such public reconciliation after the fulfillment of the public penance), 8 (Car-

subsequent legislation. Thus, the Council of Trent in its canon, which is incorporated in the Code in almost the same words,[45] in regard to the faculties of priests, limitless in extent and content, in cases of dying persons, states: "Verumtamen pie admodum, ne hac ipsa occasione aliquis pereat, in eadem Ecclesia Dei custoditum *semper* fuit, ut nulla sit reservatio in articulo mortis, atque ideo omnes sacerdotes quoslibet poenitentes a quibusvis peccatis et censuris absolvere possunt. . . ."[46] Pope Benedict XIV, in his constitution, *Pia Mater,* refers also to "the more ancient examples of ecclesiastical benignity" in the case of the dying, and expressly cites the practice at the time of St. Cyprian.[47] The members of the synod of Pistoia wondered at the extreme leniency shown by the Fathers towards dying persons. Pope Pius VI (1794), in condemning this error, cites by name the canon of Nice I, and the letters of Popes Innocent I and Celestine I in refutation. But these testimonies were mainly concerned with those who had in some way

---

thage IV, c. 76, dying persons can be publicly reconciled on the testimony of others, which is to be told them, and the public penance done on recovery), 9 (Nice I, c. 13, dying persons "*necessario vitae suae non defraudetur viatico,* but if they recover they are only to be received *sola oratione communicant*), 10 (Leo I), 12 (*reus est animarum presbiter, qui penitenciam morientibus abnegat*), 13 (Celestine I), 14 (Carthage III, c. 32, even one who commits a most public crime can be reconciled by a priest *ultima necessitas*), C. XXVI, 6.

c. 1 (in danger of death the quantity of penance is not to be imposed, but made known), 12 (*Melius est errare in misericordia remittendi quam in severitate ulciscendi,* a principle taken from St. John Chrysostom), C. XXVI, 7.

45 Sess. XIV, *De Sacr. Poen.,* cap. 7.

46 Ex Constit., *Pia Mater,* Bened. XIV, April 3, 1747, Coll., no. 361: ". . . Apostolicae caritatis Nostrae vicera dilatantes, et tam veteribus quam recentioribus ecclesiasticae benignitatis exemplis inhaerentes; siquidem extat illustre monumentum tertii Ecclesiae saeculi in epistola Sancti Cypriani, quae in novis editionibus impressa est num. XII, qua scilicet in eorum gratiam . . . et in mortis periculo versabantur . . . quo minus, ut optaverat, ad eos reconsiliandos sese conferre posset. . . ."

47 Constit., *Auctorem fidei,* August 28, 1794, error 38; the exact words are: ". . . contraria can. 13 Concilii NICAENI, decretali INNOCENTII I ad Exuperium Tolos., tum et decretali COELESTINI I ad episcopos Vienn. et Narbonen. provinciae, redolens pravitatem, quam in ea decretali sanctus Pontifex exhorret."

departed from the true faith and practice.

6. *Modern Times.*

The Reformation on the continent of Europe attacked with special vigor the sacramental system of the Church. In England, at the commencement of this movement, the essentials of the Sacraments were preserved, but later, during the reigns of Edward VI and Elizabeth, vitiated intention and Ordinals rendered the orders of their ministers invalid. On the continent of Europe, the Sacrament of Orders was attacked and eliminated by most of the Protestant sectaries from the start. Hence, they can only administer the Sacrament of Baptism validly. Schismatics have retained their belief in the seven Sacraments and valid Orders, but the Sacrament of Penance involves an exercise of jurisdiction also. There is no doubt, as already stated, that they administer Penance validly and licitly to their dying brethren. Difficulties arose in regard to heretics, due mainly to the lack of intention of receiving the Sacrament, and to schismatics, where their own minister could not be had, or they desired to have a Catholic priest. In the case of both classes of non-Catholics, the form of reconciliation and signs required were the object of several questions.

(a). *Abjuration.*—In the seventeenth century, questions were asked and responses given by the Holy See concerning the abjuration required from apostates, where its external expression meant danger to life. The Holy Office, July 25, 1630, answered that *in articulo mortis,* the confessor must absolve such a one, after making the abjuration *in foro conscientiae.*[48] Pope Benedict XIV, in his constitution, *Pia Mater,* April 5, 1747, also recognized as an ancient tradition that much less was required for the reconciliation of a dying person than one in good health.[49]

48 S. C. S. Off., July 25, 1630, Coll., no. 57.
49 Coll., no. 361.

(b). *Responses in which a sign of repentance, or a reconciliation in a very general manner suffices.*—In the nineteenth century, the Holy Office, May 9, 1821, calls attention to the fact that any *infidelis,* who gives signs of repentance, can be absolved *in articulo mortis* by any priest from any kind of sins whatsoever, and that nobody is to be then repelled from the Sacraments.[50] On July 8, 1874, the Holy Office declared that Protestants, who were also Masons, can be absolved, after exhorting them: "in genere hortentur ut se sincere subiiciant ecclesiae auctoritati, atque mandatis S. Sedis, . . ." if more cannot be demanded without danger of turning their good faith into bad.[51] In an earlier response of the Holy Office, August 1, 1855, in the case of contumacious Masons, absolution from the censure was permitted, if any *sign* of repentance had been given, on the presumption, "etiam in articulo mortis, possunt per contritionem in Dei gratiam redire, ac *internam cum membris mystici corporis Christi communicationem adipisci,*" without stating anything about the absolution from the sin. Also, in the same response, the Holy See refused to state a general rule regarding those who were members of Masonic sects, and now in ignorance and good faith, but would hardly remain thus if warned (i.e., in good faith). It did not totally exclude the possibility of omitting the warning, but left it to the prudence of the confessor, who was to be guided by approved authors and Apostolic Constitutions.[52]

(c). Responses in which there is *no mention of reconciliation.*—On July 22, 1898, the Holy Office permitted the absolution of material schismatics in good faith and provided scandal was efficaciously removed.[53]

50 S. C. S. Off., May 9, 1821, Coll., no. 757.
51 S. C. S. Off., July 8, 1874, Coll., no. 1419.
52 S. C. S. Off., August 1, 1855, Coll., no. 1116.
53 S. C. S. Off., July 20, 1898, ad 1, Coll., no. 2012.

No conditions regarding signs, nor reconciliation were attached to the response. It was not specified whether they were destitute of the senses or not. The response states that scandal must be efficaciously removed, so that full reconciliation is hardly considered. In addition, the concession of the Sacrament is refused *praeterquam in articulo mortis,* which would not be the case if full reconciliation were meant. The Holy Office, May 26, 1916, answered another question concerning schismatics, who are destitute of their senses, which has already been cited.[54] No sign of reconciliation is mentioned or demanded. It is quite clear that none in the knowledge of the minister has been given: the Sacraments are to be administered conditionally, especially *si ex adjunctis conjicere liceat, eos implicite saltem errores suos rejicere,* about which there would be no doubt if signs had been given; further, scandal is to be removed, *manifestando scilicet adstantibus (qui id nesciant) Ecclesiam supponere eos in ultimo momento ad unitatem rediisse,* but more than supposition would be had if signs had been given. Neither the question nor the response make any distinctions between those that *had* been in bad or good faith, but simply state that the Sacraments are to be given conditionally to such persons, which in our humble opinion represents the lesson of the Church's history, and is in perfect accord with the common opinion. The element of formal contumaciousness *non certe constat* in the internal forum, which judges the conscience and not the state, when the dying man is destitute of his senses. In a word, the doubt is in favor of the penitent in the internal forum. Since the particle *praesertim* is used, even this *implicit* reconciliation is not absolutely required, and the administration is permitted

54 Cfr. chapter II, *in fine.*

without any such evidence from the circumstances. The response takes for granted that the bystanders ought to know on what supposition—not moral certainty or probability—the Church is acting. The phrase *in ultimo momento* is of importance, as it refers to the time when the person is destitute of his senses, and thus cannot give any sign. This response, then, represents a restatement in somewhat more detailed manner of those of 1821, 1855, 1874, 1898, and what is, in our humble opinion, the spirit of the first five centuries, as should have already appeared, and will be further developed in the following chapters.

The Present Law.

The Code states in a general manner in canon 901 who is the subject of Penance:

> Qui post baptismum mortalia perpetravit, quae nondum per claves Ecclesiae directe remissa sunt, debet omnia quorum post diligentem sui discussionem conscientiam habeat, confiteri et circumstantias in confessione explicare, quae speciem peccati mutent.

As Baptism is a primary requisite to the reception of all other Sacraments, there is no possibility of validly receiving the Sacrament of Penance unless one has first been baptized. But theologians admit much mitigation of the other conditions in the face of approaching death. In fact, the Code contains an extremely clement canon, which governs the powers of the priest in the administration of the Sacrament to the dying:

> In periculo mortis omnes sacerdotes, licet ad confessiones non approbati, valide et licite absolvunt quoslibet poenitentes a quibusvis peccatis aut censuris, quantumvis reservatis et notoriis,

etiamsi praesens sit sacerdos approbatus, salvo praescripto can. 881, 2252.[55]

It is obvious from this canon that the Church gives full powers in connection with the Sacrament of Penance to her ministers, in order that the dying person may be helped along the road to salvation in his dying moments. The limitations contained in the final clause do not concern the subject matter of this thesis.

In a word, the present canon is an epitome of the past history. The Council of Trent had stated *nulla sit reservatio in articulo mortis,* which the present canon changes into *in periculo mortis.* But the historical antecedents of Trent lay in the early centuries, as is obvious from the condemnation of the proposition of the Pistoian synod. These early centuries were summed up in the thirteenth canon of the first ecumenical council of Nice, which was the Church's final answer to Montanism, and all the early rigorism which centered around the theory of irremissible sins, of which heresy was one. On the other hand, however, Penance is a Sacrament, and so canon 731, par. 2, must be satisfied in so far as possible. But the danger of death will, as shall appear later, considerably modify these conditions.

A. Cases of Formal Deathbed Conversions.

In cases in which the dying non-Catholic is willing to be converted, and there is plenty of time, naturally instruction should be given as fully as the circumstances will permit. This will be followed by the usual procedure contained in the Roman Ritual.[56]

55 Canon 882.

56 Cfr. *Supplementum Ritualis Romani provinciis Americae Septentrionalis Foederatae,* p. 1-6.

Past responses of the Holy See, however, clearly distinguish absolution from heresy in the external and internal forum. E. g., in the note to the Instruction S. C. de Prop. Fide, May 1, 1779, Coll., no. 533, the faculties

The canon regulating the avoidance of sacramental administrations to heretics and schismatics makes no exception for the dying.[57] It will therefore have to be fulfilled in so far as possible. The contrary custom of absolving dying heretics and schismatics, where instruction can be given, merely on the grounds that they are in good faith, and the nature of the conditional use of the Sacraments has been reprobated by the Holy See in the past.[58] The *Mens* of the same response is that as often as the dying heretic or schismatic has given some sign on which can be founded a reasonable doubt that he belongs to the Holy Catholic Church, priests will have to follow the norms laid down by approved authors. Even where danger of death is feared, in the case of an apostate, public rejection of error and

---

granted by this Congregation for parts subject to it could not be used: ". . . nec illos qui iudicialiter abiuraverint, nisi isti nati sint ubi impune grassantur haereses, et post iudicialem abiurationem illus reversi, in haeresim fuerint relapsi, et hos in foro conscientiae tantum." Much the same thing is repeated in a letter S. C. S. Off., May 7, 1882, Coll., no. 771, in which the faculty includes "haeresi externa occulta seu non deducta ad forum externum iudiciale." Again, the earlier response of S. C. de Prop. F., April 8, 1786, is cited as the norm in S. C. S. Off., March 28, 1900, Coll., no. 2079: "Non est necesse ut qui a catholica fide defecerunt, ad eamque, postmodum reverti cupiunt, publicam abiurationem praemittant, sed satis est ut *privatim* coram paucis adiurent, dummodo tamen promissa servent, ac revera abstineant communicare cum haereticis in spiritualibus, aut quidquam facere quod haeresis protestatium sit. Idem senteniendum de iis qui haeresim, in qua usque ad initio educati fuere, *privatim adiurent.*" Etc.

Hence, there is no difficulty under this head in danger of death. In the internal forum, canon 882 gives ample power, which will cover all cases. In this forum, the Church certainly does judge the occult, and the sins *sicut in conscientia.* In the external forum, however, the Church does not judge the occult, so that some sign will always be required, and the satisfaction of canon 731, no. 2, in so far as possible in an external manner. It is obvious that sometimes conflicts may arise between the Church's action through her ministers in the two fora, in which case the internal forum *qua tale* is not entirely ruled by the principles of the external forum, but depends to a large extent on the subjective conditions of the dying person. What is done in the internal forum remains within it and will not in itself be recognized in the external forum. Externally, however, what is done in the external forum is generally binding for the internal forum, unless contrary to the truth, which is known in the internal forum.

57 Canon 731, no. 2.

58 S. C. S. Off., January 13, 1864, Coll., no. 1246.

recantation were demanded if possible, and if this was not possible, these had to be made at least *in foro conscientiae.*[59] When the person is destitute of the senses, a sign would obviously likewise be necessary for complete reconciliation.

B. Cases in Which Formal Conversion Is Impossible.

Sometimes it is morally impossible to obtain any formal rejection of error, or complete reconciliation with the Catholic Church from the subject. The object of the minister should then be to secure as full a reconciliation as possible without destroying the good faith of the dying person. In the first place, prudence would suggest securing the conditions for the valid administration of the Sacraments. The Council of Trent teaches that attrition disposes one to ask for the Sacrament, and perfect contrition contains the *votum.* With these acts as basis, a general acceptance of the teaching of the Church should be forthcoming in some form. It would seem from the tenor of some of the responses of the Holy See in the past, as interpreted by theologians, points that are likely to turn the good faith of the dying man into bad can be avoided.[62] Some also permit conditional absolution, if the presence of perfect contrition is morally certain, provided more cannot be obtained. One thing is certain, that, granted perfect contrition, they are within the invisible Church: "etiam in articulo mortis possunt per contritionem in Dei gratiam redire, ac internam cum membris mystici corporis Christi communicationem adipisci. . . ."[63] But Penance, in so far as it is concerned with the absolution from the guilt of sin, pertains to the internal forum, or mystical body of the Church. Some

62 Cfr. S. C. S. Off., July 8, 1874, Coll., no. 1419; Reuter-Lehmkuhl-Umberg, *Neo-Confessarius,* no. 211.
63 S. C. S. Off., August 1, 1855, Coll., no. 1116.

distinctions, however, must be made.

(a). If the dying man lapses into unconsciousness, and is *in articulo mortis,* with moral certainty in regard to these acts, conditional absolution can certainly be given in the internal forum. Even though the dying man was contumacious, and excommunicated as such, *si clara dederint resipiscentiae signa,* which is certainly the case if perfect contrition has been manifested, absolution can also be given in the external forum.[64]

(b). If the dying man does not lapse into unconsciousness, a more express intention in regard to the Sacrament and reconciliation should be obtained. Prudence and the particular circumstances of the actual case can alone determine how this can best be done. If the dying man is a schismatic or a Protestant, who believes in the Sacrament of Penance, no difficulty need arise in this matter. Canon 731, par. 2, must also be satisfied in so far as possible. Many of the Fathers and Popes have cited the words of Our Lord: "Cast not your pearls before swine,"[65] as the scriptural basis of the refusal of the Sacraments to heretics and schismatics. But in the hypothesis, the dying man is already in internal communication with the members of Christ's mystical body, so that he is a friend of Christ, and falls in the class: "And other sheep I have, that are not of this fold: them also I must bring, and they shall hear my voice, and there shall be one fold and one shepherd."[66]

C. Cases of Those with Whom It Is Impossible to Communicate.

Under this heading, the physical impossibility must be interpreted in the sense already explained, relative

64 S. C. S. Off., August 1, 1855, Coll., no. 1116.
65 Cfr. the present chapter, no. 1.
66 John X, 16.

to Baptism.[67] The hypothesis embraces only those who are in danger of death, with added condition that definite communication is physically impossible, due to some cause either on the part of the subject or the minister, e.g., destitution of the senses, lack of knowledge of the dying man's language, etc.

(a). If some sign of sorrow, e.g., a nod, sigh, or sob, is given by the dying man, that can be interpreted as satisfying in some manner canon 731, par. 2, he may be absolved at least conditionally in virtue of canon 882. There is no reason for introducing distinctions, based on what the man *had been* in his past life. The fact is that he is probably repentant now, and the canon gives the minister full power over all sins and censures. If the man is attrite, it disposes him to ask for the Sacrament,[68] if contrite, he actually has the implicit *votum*.[69] Hence, at least conditional absolution can probably be given. Discussions as to whether these acts contain sufficient for the valid reception of the Sacrament will be reasons for the use of the conditional form, but not the refusal of absolution. The full facts are *ex hypothesi* unknown, so that the exact content or extent of such acts must remain a secret of Divine Providence, unless the sick man recovers.

(b). If the subject is already destitute of his senses and cannot even give a sign, the testimony of the bystanders can be acted on, as in the preceding case. If no sign whatever can or has been given, either by the subject himself or through others, a distinction must be introduced.

(i). The dying man, until the destitution of his

67 Cfr. chapter III, sec. B, II, 1.

68 Council of Trent, Sess. XIV, cap. 4, *De contritione*, cfr. entire chapter, which states that the *votum*: ". . . quod in illa *continetur*. . . ."

69 Ibid., l. c., "Illam vero contritionem imperfectam, quae attritio dicitur, . . . tamen eum ad Dei gratiam in *sacramento* poenitentiae *impetrandam disponit*."

senses, has not been a contumacious and formal heretic or schismatic; in which case he can certainly be absolved conditionally, as has been already demonstrated, at least with extrinsic probability.[70]

(ii). If he has been a contumacious and formal heretic or schismatic, authors disagree in their conclusions. Some say that contumacy, from its very nature, ceases in such a case.[71] Is it certain when the man has passed beyond the realm of human communication that he continues to be contumacious in the forum of conscience? The Holy Office, August 1, 1885, granted that even contumacious Masons: "etiam in articulo mortis possunt per contritionem in Dei gratiam redire, ac *internam* cum membris mystici corporis Christi communicationem adipisci. . . ."[72] But the same response introduced a distinction between the absolution in the external forum, permitting it only when *clara signa* had been given, and the internal forum. Nothing was said concerning absolution in the internal forum in such cases as are here considered. The general principle of moral theology is that the doubt is in favor of the penitent in the internal forum, and the occult is precisely the object of the judgment. In the external forum, the Church judges the manifest and not the occult. According to canon 882, the fact that the dying man *was* contumacious will not restrict the power of the priest. Hence, on the presumption that the dying man is at least attrite, and that the Church *supposes* that he was reconciled *in ultimo momento,* conditional absolution can be given.[73] Many grave authors, however, disagree with this opinion, so that the

70 Cfr., chapter II, sec. 3, B. 3.

71 Vermeersch-Creusen, II, no. 226. Cfr. chapter II, sec. 3, B.

72 Coll., no. 1116.

73 Cfr. response of May 19, 1916, cited in full in chapter II, l. c. Ita, Ferreres, *Comp Theo. Mor.,* II, ed. XII; no. 608, 7, citing Card. Gennari, *Il Monitore,* vol. 6, p. 2, p. 113, *et alii, contra plures alios.*

matter will have to be left to the prudent judgment of the minister himself. The Holy See has not condemned the milder opinion, but rather seems to implicitly include it in the response of 1916. Possibly this is also contained in St. Augustine,[74] and St. Thomas.[75]

D. Some Objections.

1. *A Response of the Holy Office.*

The Holy Office, January 13, 1864, condemned the custom of giving absolution to all dying non-Catholics, merely on account of the nature of conditional absolution, and the presumed good faith of the party, without any sign or previous act which might, even implicitly, contain a sign that the person wished to be reconciled with the Church. This silence was maintained, either through impossibility or fear of disturbing the good faith of the party. The answer was: "Usum de quo quaeritur, prout exponitur, esse improbandum." [76] It is quite clear that there is no conflict between the views expressed in the present thesis and this response. The custom, only as stated in the question is condemned, which is not at all concerned with those destitute of their senses. Further, no attempt whatsoever is made to determine the mind of the dying

74 *De adult. conjug.* cap. 28, 35: "Non ipsos enim ex hac vita arrha pacis exire velle debet mater Ecclesia." The other quotation from St. Augustine, cap. 26, 33, cited in chapter III, 3, A, 5, applies to Baptism, but St. Alphonsus, *Theo. Mor.*, VI, no. 482, and D'Annibale, *Theo. Mor.*, III, no. 317, et alii, extended it to Penance.

75 Cfr. *Suppl.*, q. viii, a. 6, which gives a principle, although from the context used by the Saint possibly only in reference to jurisdiction: ". . . sed quia necessitas legem non habet, ideo quando necessitatis articulus imminet, per Ecclesiae ordinationem non impeditur, quin absolvere possit. . . ." Again, possibly also from the context with the same restriction, Suppl., q. xx, a. 1: ". . . nisi in necessitatis articulo, ubi *nemini sacramenta* deneganda." And *Comm. in IV Lib. Sent.*, D. VI, q. 1, q. 2: ". . . et ideo si forma servetur nec aliquid exterius dicitur, quod intentionem contrariam exprimat, baptizandus est. Non enim sine causa in sacramentis necessitatis, scilicet baptismo et quibusdam aliis, actus baptizantis tam sollicite expressus est ad intentionis expressionem."

76 Coll., no. 1246.

person, or to secure a sign that might include even an implicit desire of reconciliation. The *Mens* makes it quite clear that it is only considering those who can give some sign. The later responses of 1898 and 1916 make this certain, and mention nothing concerning approved authors.

2. *Scandal.*

It is obvious from the cautions concerning the avoidance of scandal in many responses of the Holy See that there is a real danger of scandal. Oftentimes this scandal may arise from a pharisaical attitude or narrow-mindedness in charity toward dying non-Catholics. The first type can be despised; the second will be lessened greatly by protestation on the priest's part and instruction. But scandal must be avoided. Some of the responses of the Holy Office suggest a manner of doing this, e.g., on the absolution of dying Masons, July 8, 1874: "scandalum vero reparetur eo meliori modo quo fieri possit, *etiam post obitum*,'"[77] and the absolution of schismatics, who are destitute of their senses, "remoto scandalo, manifestando scilicet adstantibus (*qui id nesciant*) Ecclesiam supponere, eos *in ultimo momento* ad unitatem rediisse.'"[78] The obligation of removing scandal need offer no serious obstacle. It is one of charity, and can be removed, if possible, before the Sacraments are given. If, however, there is not time to do this, as probably the salvation of a soul is at stake, the Sacraments can be administered, and the scandal repaired afterwards. Such scandal should be out of the question among well instructed Catholics, who have tasted of the great mercy of the Master. The angels of Heaven, most pure spirits, rejoice in the repentance of one sinner

77 Coll., no. 1419.

78 S. C. S. Off., May 19, 1916, cfr. chapter II, sec. 3, B. Cfr. S. C. S. Off., July 20, 1898, Coll., no. 2012.

more than in the ninety-nine just. If there is danger of contempt of the Sacraments by the dying man's co-religionists, this can be avoided by secret administration, as far as the witnesses are concerned.[79] In the case of Penance in particular, if one destitute of the senses is given conditional absolution in the internal forum, it is hard to see that there would be an obligation of making this known to the bystanders. Where Extreme Unction is administered, manifestation cannot be avoided.

79 E. g., S. R. C., February 4, 1871, Coll., no. 1365. (Confession is today occult, so that there will be no difficulty in this case from the very nature of the Sacrament.) On the whole matter of scandal, cfr., the Instruction S. C. de Prop. F., January 30, 1807, Coll., no. 691.

CHAPTER V.

DYING NON-CATHOLICS AND THE SACRAMENTS OF HOLY VIATICUM, EXTREME UNCTION, AND CONFIRMATION.

It is naturally the desire of the priest who assists at the deathbed of a dying person to help him to the best of his ability. But each Sacrament was instituted by Christ for a definite purpose, and adds to the graces already existing in the soul. Holy Viaticum nurtures and strengthens the flame of spiritual life kindled in Baptism, after it has been dimmed by sin, and replenished in Penance; Extreme Unction[1] completes Penance and fortifies the dying person against the temptations of the devil; Confirmation marks him as a soldier of Christ. All three Sacraments, however, are aids to spiritual life already begun by the reception of Baptism. Hence, they cannot be received sacramentally until one has been validly baptized. The three Sacraments are likewise "Sacraments of the living," i.e., they must be ordinarily administered to those only who are already in the state of grace. As the theologians say, they do not primarily give "the first grace," but only *per accidens,* when it is impossible to receive the Sacrament of Penance. But surely in the hour of

1 These three Sacraments find a place in the same chapter, because the treatment of each one is somewhat similar. *Entia non sunt multiplicanda sine necessitate.* Thus, needless repetition can be avoided. Many of the arguments used in this chapter represent merely a development of ideas touched on in earlier chapters. If the writer has perhaps been guilty of some repetition, this has been done for the sake of clarity and completeness of presentation. The argument in history from the second chapter to the end of the present one forms one whole, which tends to bring out the force of the preliminary consideration in chapter II, sec. 3, B, 1.

death, Penance will also have to be used, wherever this is possible. The order prescribed by the Roman Ritual is Penance, Holy Viaticum, and Extreme Unction.[3]

Other circumstances, however, have to be taken into consideration, e.g., the attainmnet of the use of reason, the necessary knowledge, and intention, etc. As these are somewhat similar in the cases of Holy Viaticum and Extreme Unction, the two Sacraments can well find treatment in the same chapter. Further, the historical evidence in the case of Extreme Unction is somewhat scant, possibly due to the fact that it is implicitly contained in that regarding dying persons and the Sacrament of Penance. More could be adduced for the Sacrament of Holy Viaticum, but again much depends on the interpretation of uncertain terminology. The question is less practical in regard to the Sacrament of Confirmation, as this is now regularly reserved to the Bishop. In the foreign missions, however, the Holy See has granted and continues to grant special faculties to priests. Hence, occasion may arise to use them in cases of dying non-Catholics.

1. Historical Survey.

1. *Holy Viaticum in the First Five Centuries.*

It is very difficult to draw any definite conclusions from the testimonies of the early centuries concerning the administration of Holy Communion to the dying. Historians admit there is a comparative silence on the subject of secret confession, as distinguished from public confession, although they recognize that a difference must be drawn between the conditions and formalities required for the one and not the other.[4] The Council of Trent, however, distinctly teaches:

---

3 Tit. V, cap. 1, *De Sacr. Ext. Unct.*, no. 2 (Romae, 1913).

4 Cfr. chapter IV. Pesch, *Prae. Theo. Dogm.*, VII, nos. 263-269, who cites many authorities, and Tanquerey, *Syn. Theo. Mor.*, I, *Pars Dogmatica*, nos. 61-67.

". . . unde cum a sanctissimis, et antiquissimis, patribus, magno, unanimique consensu, secreta confessio sacramentalis, *qua ab initio Ecclesia sancta est, et modo etiam utitur,* fuerit semper commendata. . ."[5] The crux of the difficulty, in reference to the dying, is the conceded uncertainty of the meaning of the early terminology, and distinction between partial and complete reconciliation.

It can be stated with certainty that the Blessed Eucharist was regarded as a symbol of unity from the very earliest times.[6] As there is one body of Christ, the Church, all must be in this to receive the Body and Blood of Christ, thus, for example, in the Didache.[7] St. Ignatius writes that those in schism do not communicate in Holy Communion,[8] and St. Justin that it is not lawful for anyone to Communicate if he does not believe "what we teach."[9] This notion of the Blessed Eucharist is based directly on Sacred Scripture by St. John Chrysostom,[10] and St. Augustine.[11]

St. Cyprian seems, however, to draw a distinction between public reconciliation and some other form, which is incomplete and does not permit the reception of the Holy Eucharist.[12] Thus, he complains that pub-

5 Sess. XIV, cap. 5, *de confessione.*

6 Cfr. chapter IV, note (2).

7 IX, 4, 5, R. de J., no. 6.

8 *Phil.* III, 2, 3; IV; V; R. de J., nos. 56-57.

9 *Apol.* I, 66, R. de J., no. 66.

10 *In Jo., hom.* 146, 2 and 3, where Ephs., V, 30, is cited, MPG, 59, 260: *In Ep. I ad Cor.,* hom. 24, 2, MPG, 61, 200.

11 *Sermo* 227 cites I Cor. X, 17, MPL, 38, 1099; *In Jo* XXVI, 13, MPL, 35, 1012.

12 In *Ep.* XV, 1 (CSEL, 3, p. 514), (ANF, V, p. 291, *Ep.* X, 1), the main point of complaint is: ". . . offerre pro illis et eucharistiam (dare) id est sanctum Domini Corpus profanare audeant. . . ." In *Ep.* XVI, 2 (CSEL, 3, p. 518-519), (ANF, V, p. 290, *Ep.* IX, 2) St. Cyprian again objects: ". . . et per manus impositionem episcopi et cleri jus communicationis accipiant . . . ad communicationem admittuntur, et offertur nomine eorum, et nondum paenitentia acta, nondum exomologesi facta, nondum manu eis ab episcopo et clero imposita eucharistia illis datur, cum scriptum est, . . ." and quotes I Cor. XI, 27. Ibid., 3: ". . . ante extitum persecutionis metum, ante reditum

lic penitents are admitted: ". . . while the penitence is not yet performed, confession is not yet made, the hands of the bishop and clergy are not yet laid upon them, the Eucharist is given to them."[13] Again, St. Cyprian states that he withholds public peace for disciplinary reasons, and also because the lapsed could cure it by means of voluntary martyrdom, if they wished.[14] Those who had not obtained certificates from the martyrs must wait "for public peace,"[15] which could be granted by a deacon in cases of necessity.[16] He also bitterly complained that the ministers of the Church had received the oblations before this complete and public reconciliation took place.[17] At the outset the saint seems to have refused public reconciliation and consequently Holy Communion, even to the lapsed who repented and were in a dying condition.[18] But the authorities of Rome ordered: ". . . if any who may have fallen into this temptation begin to be taken with sickness and repent of what they have done, and desire communion, it should be certainly granted them. . . ."[19] St. Cyprian accepted this mandate, and later condemned the denial of reconcilia-

nostrum, ante ipsum paene martyrium excessum communicent cum lapsis et offerant et eucharistiam tradunt. . . ." And *Ep.* XVII, 2 (CSEL, 3, p. 522): ". . . quo magis in his gravissimis et extremis delictis caute omnia et moderate secundum disciplinam Domini observari oportet." Cfr. *Ep.* XV, 2, 3 (CSEL, 3, p. 514-515), (ANF, V, p. 291, *Ep.* X, 1); *Ep.* LVII, 2 (CSEL, 3, p. 651-652), (ANF, V, p. 337), where St. Cyprian orders the Blessed Eucharist to be given as a sign to those publicly reconciled outside of danger of death.

13 *Ep.* X, 1 (ANF, V, p. 291), (CSEL, 3, p. 517, *Ep.* XV, 1).

14 *Ep.* XIII, 2 (ANF, V, p. 293-294), (CSEL, 3, p. 525-526, *Ep.* XIX, 2).

15 *Ep.* XIII, 2 cfr. note (14); *Ep.* XII, 1 (ANF, V, p. 293), (CSEL, V, p. 523-524, *Ep.* XVIII, 1).

16 *Ep.* XII, 1 (ANF, V, p. 293), (CSEL, 3, p. 523-525, *Ep.* XVIII, 1).

17 Cfr. note (12) to this chapter.

18 *Ep.* II, 2 (ANF, V, p. 280-281), (CSEL, 3, p. 486-487, *Ep.* VIII, 2).

19 *Ep.* II, 3 (ANF, V, p. 281), (CSEL, 3, p. 487-488, *Ep.* VIII, 3). Cfr. *Ep.* XIII, 2 (ANF, V, p. 293-294), (CSEL, 3, p. 525-526, *Ep.* XIX, 2); *Ep.* XIV (ANF, V, p. 294-295), (CSEL, 3, p. 527-529, *Ep.* XX).

tion to any dying person as that of Novatians, who were also themselves included in this mercy: "And yet to these persons themselves repentance is granted, and the hope of lamenting and atoning is left . . . no one is to be restrained from the fruit of satisfaction and the hope of peace, . . . since God exhorts "both that sinners are brought back to repentance, and that pardon and mercy are not denied to penitents.'"[20] Absolutely none are to be refused.[21] Even those that are fleeing from persecution, who "shall fall by chance among thieves, or shall die in fever and in weakness." If such a one "dies without peace and communion . . ." it will be before God . . ."inactive negligence and cruel hardness. . . .'"[22] In conclusion, St. Cyprian carefully distinguished the obstinate from the less guilty,[23] recognized a state of secret or occult reconciliation, which his priests in Carthage improperly considered as sufficient for the reception of Holy Communion. The saint does not object to this secret reconciliation, but vigorously denies that it is sufficient for the restoration of public communion, which is an essential requisite for the reception of Holy Communion, and begins after the public absolution by the bishop. At first, he does not seem to have permitted public reconciliation even to the dying without the proper formalities, but later, through the interception of Rome, admitted all on the point of death.

The councils of Elvira (306), Arles (314), and Nice I

20 *Ep.* LI, 26, 29 (ANF, V, p. 334), (CSEL, 3, 632-638, *Ep.* LV, 12, 15, 17, 19, 26, 29); Cfr. *Ep.* LI, 12 (ANF, V, p. 330), and 15, 17, 19 (ANF, V, p. 331-332).

21 *Ep.* LI, 26, 29 (ANF, V, p. 334-335), (CSEL, 3, p. 644-647, *Ep.* LV, 26, 29).

22 *Ep.* LIII, 3, 5 (ANF, V, p. 337-338), (CSEL, 3, 652-654, *Ep.* LVII, 3, 5).

23 Cfr. *Ep.* LIV, 1, 15 (ANF, V, p. 338-339, 344-345), (CSEL, 3, p. 666-667, 684-685, *Ep.* LIX, 1, 15). *Ep.* LI, 29 (ANF, V, p. 335), (CSEL, 3, p. 647, *Ep.* LV). *Ep.* LII, 2 (ANF, V, p. 336), (CSEL, 3, p. 648-649, *Ep.* LVI).

(325), will scarcely yield any more definite historical data. The council of Elvira stated that only a bishop could receive a public penitent into the Church, i.e., probably formally and publicly, but in case of necessity, a priest or deacon could give such a one Communion as a sign of this reconciliation.[24] This is likewise referred to as an ancient custom. Some have attempted to explain this canon by saying that it was never put into practice,[25] others on the ground that absolution was not given. However, if we distinguish secret absolution (*a culpa*) from public (*a poena*), there is no difficulty, and presume that some occult form of reconciliation has been given antecedently, or is given before the administration of Communion by the priest. The council of Arles orders that Communion is not to be given to apostates, even on their deathbeds, unless they recover, and do fruits worthy of penance.[26] Nothing is said concerning secret absolution or reconciliation, and hence it is not excluded. The ecumenical council of Nice I (325), as has been stated in a previous chapter,[27] orders the *Viaticum* to be given to all dying persons. Some maintain that this word means absolution alone, others absolution and Communion. Whatever may be the truth in the matter, it certainly permits some concession that did not involve full public reconciliation, which the same canon orders is not to be given until some public penance, although considerably modified, has been undergone. The final sentence of the same canon also expressly states that the Holy Eucharist is not to be ad-

24 c. 32, Hef.-Lecq., I, p. 238.

25 Cfr. Pesch, *Prae. Theo. Dogm.*, VII, no. 48, who cites various authorities. Cfr. also Ibid., op. c., no. 263-269.

26 c. 22, Mansi, 2, 469.

27 The entire argument in the historical sections should now be drawn together. The simple statement is found in chapter II, sec. 3, B, preliminary consideration 1. It reappears in chapter IV, in which note (2) is of particular interest, and the entire second section. In the present section it is finally developed.

ministered to dying persons, unless they ask for It, and the bishop decides that they should be given It.[28] Hence, it would seem that formal conversion was necessary for public reconciliation in the complete sense even for the dying and the reception of Holy Communion. This opinion is likewise in conformity with the testimonies of the Fathers, and the attitude of St. Cyprian, that the Blessed Eucharist is a special bond of public unity with the body of the Church. In the fifth century this becomes especially evident.

A. The Holy Viaticum.

2. *The Fifth Century to Modern Times.*

While the bishop was the ordinary minister of public reconciliation, it was recognized that an exception had to be made for dying persons, even in the times of St. Cyprian. This becomes clearer in the ecumenical council of Nice I. In the second council of Carthage, it was regulated that a priest could reconcile a penitent (i.e., public) in case of necessity when the bishop was hindered.[29] Pope Innocent I (405) wrote that at no time was penance ever refused to the dying, although Holy Communion was not conceded. Now he orders *extrema communio* to be given to all who ask for It.[30] In France, the abuse of denying the Sacrament to those condemned to death existed from about this time as a civil penalty, according to some.[31] At all events, Pope Celestine I (422-432) condemned the refusal of penance (it is not certain whether this is private or public) to any dying person who asked for

28 c. 13, Hef.-Lecq., I, p. 417. Cfr. Pesch, op. c., no. 51. The final words of the canon are: "Generaliter autem omni cuilibet in exitu posito et poscenti sibi communionis gratiam tribui, episcopus probabiliter ex oblatione dare debebit," which seems to refer to a formal public Communion in connection with the public formal reconciliation.

29 c. 4, Mansi, III, 691.

30 Denz., no. 95.

31 Cfr. Pesch, *Prae. Theo. Dogm.*, VII, no. 57.

it, but without any mention of Holy Communion.[32] Pope Felix (487) ordered that ordained clerics who had received rebaptism, regarded as an heretical practice, were to be excluded, and only *in articulo mortis* admitted to lay Communion; the lower clergy and laity were to undergo a long process of public penance, but if they died earlier, the Viaticum (in our sense of the term) is not to be refused to them.[33] If, however, they recover, and have been admitted to Communion merely because of sickness, they must complete the penance in the highest degree of penitents, in accordance with the canon of Nice I. These enactments were probably drawn up to meet the special crime of rebaptism and suppress the practice. This was regarded as heretical, and the legislation in question may be taken as hardly any stricter than the general practice in regard to dying heretics. A council of Agde (506) orders that *extrema communio* (which is obviously used in our sense of the term Viaticum [34]) is not to be refused to anyone who is near death.

B. *Extreme Unction.*—The first clear testimony outside of the Sacred Scriptures, concerning the administration of Extreme Unction is contained in a letter of Pope Innocent I (416), which gives the Roman practice. The oil used is to be blessed by the bishop, but the Sacrament can be administered by any priest in cases of necessity. It must not be given to anyone to whom the other Sacraments have been refused: "Nam paenitentibus istud infundi non potest, quia genus est Sacramenti. Nam quibus reliqua sacramenta negantur, quomodo unum genus putatur posse concedi?"[35]

---

32 Denz., no. 111.

33 Hef.-Lecq., II, p. 934-935.

34 Agde (506); c. 63, D. I., Cfr. Innocent I, who uses the same term *extrema communio* in a passage in which there is no doubt as to the meaning, Denz., no. 95.

35 Denz., no. 99. Cfr. Pesch, op. c., VII, no. 514, who rejects the interpretation of the passage so as to mean Confirmation instead of

It is clear from these words that this Sacrament can only be given to the penitent after public reconciliation, as a later testimony, under Pope Leo IV (850), explains: "Hoc tamen sciendum, quia, si is, qui infirmatur, publicae poenitentiae mancipatus est, non potest huius mysterii consequi medicinam, nisi prius reconciliatione percepta communionem corporis et sanguinis Christi meruerit. Cui enim reliqua sacramenta interdicta sunt, hoc uno nulla ratione uti conceditur."[36] This is in perfect harmony with the rule found in the Roman Ritual today, that the ordinary procedure is Penance, Holy Viaticum, and then Extreme Unction. If Holy Viaticum cannot be administered, then the order will be Penance and Extreme Unction. This follows from the fact that Extreme Unction is a Sacrament of the living. It is illogical to teach that conditional Extreme Unction should be administered without conditional absolution, if the latter is possible, and the subject is probably not in the state of grace. It is interesting to note also, that Extreme Unction pertains to the external forum, as the second testimony clearly demonstrates.[37] Any other interpretation would lead to the absurd conclusion, that all the Sacraments in these times were refused to penitents and dying Catholics, although public penitents.

The statutes of St. Boniface speak in the same gen-

Extreme Uunction (*fortasse*). The latter interpretation does not seem probable, as the parties in question are adults, since they are undergoing public penance, which was only imposed on adults. If so, there is no reason for supposing that they had not already been confirmed.

36 Denz., no. 315 (c. 8, *Counc. Ticinense*, 850); Mansi, 14, 932.

37 Cfr. Tanquerey, *Syn. Theo. Dogm.*, III, no. 779: "Extrema Uunctio remittit etiam *poenam temporalem* peccato debitam, non quidem totam, sed juxta gradum dispositionis in subjecto existente," which is the common teaching. But the remission of the *poena* as distinct from the *culpa* involved the external forum and at least the promise of public penance. Cfr. also Pope Leo I (440-461), in the letter *Magna indign.*, Denz., no. 145: ". . . Sufficit enim illa confessio, quae primum Deo offertur, tum etiam sacerdoti, qui quo delictis poenitentium precator accredit. Tunc enim demum plures ad poenitentiam poterunt provocari, si populi auribus non publicetur conscientia confitentis."

eral terms of giving Penance, the Holy Viaticum, and annointing dying persons, without any special reference to their past lives.[38]

C. *Conclusions.*—From the time of Pope Innocent I, public reconciliation, Holy Viaticum, and Extreme Unction, seem to have been regulated by the same rule, and where one was given the others were also. As has already been stated,[39] definite signs, or at least a voluntary undertaking seems to have been required for the infliction of public penance, and consequent public reconciliation. As regards the internal forum, nothing can be stated with certainty, even in cases concerning persons who had been Catholics all their lives. In cases of destitution of the senses, the problem is likewise the same. It is certain that the Church vigorously repudiated all attempts at rigorism. Possibly the distinctions between absolution *a culpa* and *a poena,* and the external and internal forum, may permit piercing through this curtain of historical uncertainty. The conjectures are at least worthy of consideration, when one remembers that the problem cannot be restricted to dying non-Catholics alone, but all classes who do not give some signs, either through another or in their state of destitution.

The main questions in regard to Extreme Unction, until comparatively recent times, centered around the institution and not the administration of this Sacrament, with which the present thesis is not concerned. St. Thomas's practical teaching that the Sacraments must not be denied *in articulo mortis,* which has already been cited, is merely the conclusion of history, in the

38 c. 18, 31 (clearly distinguishes between the cases of the normal and the dying, who are to be reconciled without delay and given the Holy Eucharist), 32 (a sick man can be given immediate reconciliation on the testimony of others, with the Holy Eucharist; *if he recovers these witnesses must tell him what has been done*), Hef.-Lecq., III, p. 931-932.

39 Cfr. chapter IV.

humble opinion of the writer.

3. Modern times.

It is not until the eighteenth century, that responses contain matter specifically concerned with dying non-Catholics and these Sacraments.

The Holy Office, May 10, 1703, prescribed that the Viaticum should not be administered to a dying adult neophyte, unless he at least distinguished the spiritual food from the corporal, knowing and believing in the Real Presence. Extreme Unction could not be conferred on such a dying neophyte, unless he had at least some intention of receiving it *in beneficium animae pro mortis tempore ordinatam.*[40] This is cited in a response to a similar question by the Congregation of the Propaganda Fidei, September 26, 1821.[41] In a response of the Holy Office, May 9, 1821, concerning *recidivi* and *consuetudinarii* in general, the missionary is told to consult approved authors. A caution is, however, added that any priest can absolve *quemlibet fidelium,* from any kind of censure or sin, if he gives signs of repentance *in articulo mortis;* "et neminem tunc repelli a participatione Sacramentorum, nempe Extremae Unctionis, si aegrotent, et SSmi Viatici, nisi quoad Viaticum obiciatur consuetudo, qua iis qui extremo supplicio mox punientur denegatur, de qua quidem consuetudine nihil hic pronunciatur."[42] The latter response concerns habitual formal sinners, but the wording is quite general. On April 10, 1861, the Holy Office warned in a response that the Sacraments of Confirmation and Extreme Unction are not to be administered to dying neophytes, unless they have a minimum of knowledge and proper intention. That this is not very much is clear, as the same response admonishes the mission-

40 Coll., no. 256, ad 8.
41 Coll., no. 768.
42 Coll., no. 757.

ary to instruct the sick person more diligently when he recovers in the mysteries of faith, and the nature and effects of the Sacraments.[43]

The element of scandal also received attention. The practice of the missionaries of giving Extreme Unction to all the sick whom they believed in danger was commended. In cases, however, in which the Sacrament was administered in the presence of heretics, this was only tolerated, if it did not expose the Sacrament to their contempt.[44] In 1871, the Congregation of Rites gave permission for the occult administration (i. e., as regards outsiders) of the Holy Communion to the sick (*Deferendi . . . occulte ad infirmos . . .*) without vestments or lights, if there was danger from heretics or schismatics. The same concession was granted for Extreme Unction.[45] In 1906, with the approbation of the Pope, the brief form of Extreme Unction was permitted *in casu verae necessitatis*.[46] In the 1916 response, concerning schismatics, who are destitute of the senses, already cited several times, Extreme Unction was expressly mentioned and included. Hence, it can be administered conditionally, under all such circumstances, after absolution.[47]

Confirmation.—This Sacrament has already been touched on in an earlier chapter in a somewhat different connection. Particular difficulties arose in the case of Confirmation administered by schismatics. Pope Benedict XIV ordered that it should not be administered in the Western Church, until such an age as the subjects would understand the difference between this Sacrament and Baptism, and that it made them soldiers

43 S. C. S. Off., April 10, 1861, Coll., no. 1213. Cfr. S. C. de Prop. F., September 26, 1821, Coll., no. 768, which refers to the older response S. C. S. Off., May 10, 1703, ad 8, Coll., no. 256.

44 S. C. S. Off., December 11, ad 17 et 18, 1850, Coll., no. 1054.

45 S. R. C., February 4, 1871, Coll., no. 1365.

46 S. C. S. Off., April 25, 1906, Coll., no. 2233.

47 Cfr. chapter II, sec. 3, B.

of Christ, but said nothing concerning cases of necessity.[48] In 1854, the Congregation of the Council called attention to the fact that the subject did not have to be so old for Confirmation as for First Communion.[49]

The contacts with schismatics also gave rise to the question as to whether Confirmation administered by their priests should be repeated. The general principle was laid down by the Holy Office, July 5, 1853, that it was not expedient to repeat Confirmation conferred by schismatics, even though the minister had been a priest, unless the faculty had been expressly withdrawn. On this basis, it was stated that this faculty had been withdrawn in Bulgaria, Cyprus, Italy, and the adjacent Islands, but not in Valachia, Moldavia, or Asia, where it had been acquiesced in.[50] In subsequent responses for Constantinople and Jerusalem, it was declared that repetition was not expedient, except in cases of persons to be promoted to Tonsure or Sacred Orders, and then only secretly and *conditionally*.[51] Later, certain schismatics introduced a custom of using a *pennicillum,* and so the responses were given that Confirmation was not to be repeated, except as above, or at the request of the parents, and not unless after investigation it was discovered that this instrument was used. In such cases, it is to be repeated *conditionally* and secretly.[52]

4. General Appreciation.

The apparent lack of explicit testimony concerning the internal forum and occult reconciliation of dying persons ought not to cause much surprise. The *disciplina arcani* might to some extent explain this. The

---

48 Const., *Eo quamvis tempore,* May 4, 1745, Coll., no. 352.

49 S. C. Coun., November 19, 1854, Coll., no. 1105.

50 Coll., no. 1095.

51 Litt. S. C. S. Off., March 16, 1872, Coll., no. 1381 (Jerusalem); S. C. S. Off., April 2, 1879, Coll., no. 1515 (Constantinople).

52 S. C. S. Off., January 14, 1885, Coll., no. 1630 (Jerusalem).

letters of St. Cyprian emphasize the need of maintaining rigorous discipline by an insistance on severe public penances, and excluding the hope of public reconciliation until these should be completed. As he says himself any hastiness or teaching of easier methods would work much harm. But, the saint does not attempt to regulate occult reconciliation, although he clearly supposes its possibility. Even in modern times, much of what takes place within this internal forum is left largely to moral theology, or rather to the prudence of the minister as guided by the principles of this science. Oftentimes, in such questions, the Holy See has refused to state a general law,[52] but rather directed the petitioner to consult approved authors.[53] The science of moral theology was in embryonic stage in these early centuries, so that such occult reconciliation pertained to the prudence of the individual minister. The silence is, however, not absolute.[54]

It would seem that the Sacraments of Holy Viaticum and Extreme Unction pertained to the external forum, and so demanded public reconciliation before they could be received. This public reconciliation is quite distinct from absolution *a culpa* or secret confession, and could not be given to even the dying unless they either formally converted, or gave some sign, or witnesses were present. But it is possible for a deacon, in the absence of a bishop or priest to grant the dying man this public

---

53 E. g., Instr. S. C. de Prop. F, April 17, 1777, ad X, Coll., no. 522, but with the principle in VI, *Doctores opiniones ad Ecclesiae decreta sunt exigendae, non ipsa decreta ad opinantium libitum inflectenda.* S. C. S. Off., August 1, 1855, Coll., no. 1116; S. C. S. Off., September 6, 1899, Coll., no. 2068, final solution left to the prudence of the missionary. Cfr. S. C. S. Off., September 18, 1850, Coll., no. 1050 S. C. Off., July 6, 1898, ad. 2, Coll., no. 2007, consult approved authors. In another connection the opinions of Ballerini, Genicot, D'Annibale, and Bucceroni, could be followed with a safe conscience, S. Poen., January 9, 1899, Coll., no. 2031 Quoted specifically. Cursory glances at the various constitutions of Pope Benedict XIV show what an important role the opinions of authorities play.

54 Cfr. Chapter IV, sec. 2, chapter V, sec. 2, 1, 2.

reconciliation, which again proves that it cannot be confused with absolution *a culpa*.[55] Before the Council of Nice I, it seems likewise quite clear that this public reconciliation was sometimes granted, but the Holy Eucharist refused, for disciplinary reasons.[56] In the Council of Nice I, three distinct stages are recognized; first, the giving of the *viaticum* (the meaning of which is not clear) to all dying persons, without any reference as to whether they asked for it or not; secondly, after recovery the inception of public penance, after the completion of which, complete reconciliation would take place; and thirdly, the giving of the Holy Eucharist only to those dying persons who asked for It, and by the judgment of the bishop. In the fifth century, it is quite certain, that public reconciliation and the Holy Eucharist were refused to no dying person who requested them, either expressly, if in control of his senses, or through signs given through the testimony of others, if destitute of his senses; but there had to be witnesses to the public reconciliation. In the seventh century, others were taking the *votum poenitentiae* for the dying man without his knowledge, and when he was destitute of his senses. The difficulty seems to have been, that public penance could not be imposed apart from the will of the subject, or at least without witnesses who would inform the sick man of his obligations on recovery. The Sacraments of Holy Viaticum and Extreme Unction could not be given unless this public act had taken place, because they were looked on as both pertaining to the external forum. The evidences show this clearly in so far as Extreme Unction is denied to an unreconciled public penitent.

---

55 St. Cyprian, *Ep.* XVIII (ANF, V, p. 297). Cfr. Pesch, op. c., VII, no. 265, 415.

56 Cfr. chapter IV, sec. 1, and the present chapter.

5. General Application to the Code.

A comparison of the general canons of the Code concerning Penance, the Blessed Eucharist, and Extreme Unction reflects these historical appreciations.

Penance Canon 901.	Holy Eucharist Canon 853	Extreme Unction Canon 943.
Qui post baptismus mortalia perpetravit, quae nondum per claves Ecclesiae directe remissa sunt, debet omnia quorum post diligentem sui discussionem conscientiam habeat, confiteri et circumstantias in confessione explicare, quae speciem peccati mutent.	Quilibet baptizatus qui *iure* non prohibetur, admitti potest et debet ad sacram communionem.	Infirmis autem qui, cum suae mentis compotes essent, illud *saltem implicite petierunt aut verisimiliter petiissent,* etiamsi deinde sensus vel usum rationis amiserint, nihilominus absolute praebeatur.
Canon 870.		
In poenitentiae sacramento, per indicialem absolutionem a legitimo ministro impertitam, *fideli rite disposito* remittuntur peccata post baptismum commissa.		
Canon 882	Canon 885.	Canon 942.
In periculo mortis *omnes sacerdotes,* licet ad confessiones non approbati, valide et licite absolvunt *quoslibet poenitentes a quibusvis peccatis aut censuris, quantumvis reservatis et notoriis,* etiamsi praesens sit sacerdos approbatus. . . .	1. Arcendi sunt ab Eucharistia *publice indigni, quales sunt excommunicati, interdicti manifestoque infames, nisi de eorum poenitentia et emendatione constet* et *publico scandalo* prius satisfecerint.	Hoc sacramentum non est conferendum illis qui *impoenitentes in manifesto peccato mortali contumaciter perseverant;* quod si hoc dubium fuerit, conferatur sub conditione.

The Blessed Eucharist, as is manifest from the history and the canons of the Code, is especially a Sacrament of the external forum. Any baptized person who is not prohibited by the law can and must be admitted to Holy Communion. But all heretics and schismatics are juridically excluded by canon 731, par. 2, and regarded in the external forum as under censure. Thus, in cases of formal conversion, the ordinary procedure involves conditional Baptism, if necessary, absolution from censure, and finally conditional absolution in the internal forum.[57] They are to be repelled from the Holy Eucharist who are publicly unworthy, such are excommunicated, interdicted and those manifestly *infames,* unless it is clear concerning their penitence and emendation and they shall have repaired public scandal in the first place. Now, the heretics and schismatics in question were in the state of heresy or schism, so that the Church does not renew public relationship with them until there is some definite sign given. Hence, there can be no question of administering the Blessed Eucharist, unless there is some form of external conversion, or some clear sign. This view is confirmed by an instruction of the Holy Office, August 1, 1855, concerning contumacious Masons. Although it was conceded that internal reconciliation to the mystical Body of Christ was possible, absolution from the censure and ecclesiastical burial were permitted only: ". . . si clara dederint resipiscentiae signa (quae passim a doctoribus enumerantur), possunt etiam post mortem ab ecclesiastica censura absolvi. . . ."[58] No reference is made to the internal forum. Hence, it would seem that positive signs of reconciliation are necessary for the administration of the Holy Eucharist, even where belief in the Real Presence is certain.

In the case of the Holy Eucharist, a minimum of knowledge and belief is absolutely demanded, which can hardly be postulated, except in the cases of schismatics and some High Church Anglicans. In danger

57 Cfr. S. C. S. Off., July 20, 1859, Coll., no. 1178; *Supplementum Ritualis Romani pro provinciis Americae Septentrionalis Foederatae,* p. 1-6.

58 Coll., no. 1116.

of death, it is enough for children: "ut sciant Corpus Christi a communi cibo discernere illudque reverenter adorare."[59] But with the two exceptions mentioned, even this minimum cannot be postulated for such dying persons. Hence, in their cases, some instruction would seem to be absolutely necessary, and something more than signs, which will suffice for the administration of the other Sacraments. The due reverence for the Sacraments of Baptism, Confirmation, Penance, and Extreme Unction can be protected by the use of the conditional form, which is impossible in the case of the Holy Eucharist.

The Sacrament of Extreme Unction is the complement of the Sacrament of Penance. Ordinarily, the latter removes the guilt of mortal sin, and must be received before the former, which purifies the senses and eradicates the remains of sin. Extreme Unction only restores the soul accidentally to a state of grace when it has been lost and not revivified by Penance. From this viewpoint it is illogical, and contrary to the prescription of the Ritual, to teach that absolution should be denied, but Extreme Unction conceded. In cases in which there is some form of conversion, or signs have been given, there will be no difficulty. But suppose there are no signs, and none can be obtained, through the physical impossibility of communication? Theologians commonly teach that at least conditional Extreme Unction can be administered, even in cases in which conditional absolution has been refused. The reasons adduced are: First, an habitual intention suffices for the validity of Extreme Unction; and, secondly, no sensible sign is necessary, but attrition will suffice.[60] It seems strange that provided some inten-

59 Canon 855, no. 1.

60 Pesch, *Prae. Theo. Dogm.*, VII, no. 86 (in fine). Vermeersch, *Theo. Mor.*, III, no. 599. Cfr. chapter II, sec. 3.

tion is postulated this should be restricted in the actual case, which is for the most part unknown and a mystery of Divine Providence. If there is such an intention, why should it not grow under the influence of Divine grace to sufficiency for the administration of conditional absolution? The second reason applies equally to cases of dying Catholics. But there is no doubt that the custom has always prevailed of giving such at least conditional absolution as well as Extreme Unction.

As a final conclusion, the following statements would seem to be warranted. There can be no question of administering the Holy Eucharist without the fulfillment of canon 731, par. 2, in some rather express manner. The history entirely agrees with this conclusion. But, with the disappearance of public penance, Extreme Unction seems to have been stressed as the complement of Penance, although quasi-external. Theologians also consider the possibilities of the valid reception of Extreme Unction as much greater than that of Penance. It is not until the response of 1916, however, that this Sacrament receives express mention by the Holy See in connection with dying heretics and schismatics, and then it is placed on the same basis with conditional absolution for practical purposes. In the cases of neophytes, the Holy See permits the administration of Extreme Unction and Confirmation, but emphasizes the need of some instruction, even for the dying, and a spiritual intention, but nothing is stated for cases in which this is impossible. Holy Viaticum, by its very nature, demands a knowledge and belief in the Real Presence.

3. The Present Law.

(As much has been said already which logically falls under this section, the points will be briefly summarized).

A. The Young.

In danger of death, it is enough that the recipients know how to distinguish the Body of Christ from common food and reverently adore It, that the most holy Eucharist can and must be administered to children.[61] Extreme Unction can only be conferred on a *fidelis,* who is in danger of death on account of old age or sickness after the use of reason has been attained.[62]

It is quite clear from the Code itself that a bare minimum of knowledge is demanded from the dying child for the reception of the Blessed Eucharist, which is much less than is required under other circumstances.[63] Both the Sacrament of Penance and Extreme Unction demand either the possibility of committing actual sin after the reception of Baptism, or for the latter at least the possibility of temptation. But one who has never attained the use of reason, in the sense already explained,[64] is not capable of actual sin or temptation. Further, in his case, not even the secondary end of the Sacrament of Extreme Unction can be attained, namely, strengthening against the temptations of the devil.

Although the administration of the Sacrament of Confirmation is suitably in the Latin Church deferred to about the seventh year of age, nevertheless it can only be conferred before this age, if the infant is in danger of death, or it seems expedient to the minister for grave and just causes.[65] Hence, this Sacrament can be conferred on such dying *infantes,* if this is possible. As the parents in question are non-Catholics,

61 Canon 854, no. 2.
62 Canon 940, no. 1.
63 Canon 854, no. 2.
64 Cfr. this chapter, sec. 1; chapter II, sec. 1; chapter III, sec. 2.
65 Canon 788.

however, this will hardly be feasible, in view of what has already been said concerning the prudence to be exercised, even in the case of Baptism. If the parents were willing to have the infant baptized in any case, and the minister has the necessary faculties, the infant should be confirmed.

B. Adults.

1. *Holy Viaticum.*

In cases of formal conversion, there is not much difficulty. Some instruction will, however, have to be given, that the dying person may know and believe in the Real Presence, and adore the Blessed Sacrament.[66]

When formal conversion is impossible, but a sign is given, some distinctions must be introduced. If the dying person was a member of a schism or sect that believed in the Real Presence, Holy Viaticum will obviously be administered. But in the case of others, the general attitude of Protestantism, which denies the Real Presence, must be taken into consideration. Hence, some instruction to supply the minimum of knowledge is necessary, which can be given if action is taken on a personal sign of the dying man. If the priest is acting on the testimony of others, he will have to find out from them whether the dying man has the necessary knowledge or not. This will be true also in Christian surroundings in cases in which the dying person is baptized for the first time, and has probably attained the use of reason.

In case the subject is destitute of the senses, and no sign can be obtained, it does not seem that the Holy Eucharist can be administered. This will also be true where the dying person certainly believed in the Real

66 Canon 854, no. 2. This rule was applied to dying adults, S. C. S. Off., May 10, 1703, ad 8, Coll., no. 256, and in greater detail, S. C. S. Off., April 10, 1861, ad 1, Coll., no. 1213.

Presence. Contumacy may not be manifest under such circumstances, but this is not required that a person be excluded from the reception of Holy Communion. Even after the administration of conditional absolution, the dying man is publicly regarded in the external forum of the Church as *excommunicatus*.[67] The Church in her external forum does not judge of the occult or purely internal, and rules out all evidence taken from the internal forum. But they are to be repelled from the Holy Eucharist who are publicly unworthy, excommunicated, interdicted and those manifestly *infames,* unless it is clear concerning their penitence and emendation and they shall have repaired public scandal.[68]

2. *Extreme Unction.*

Where conditional absolution has been granted, there will clearly be little difficulty concerning Extreme Unction. What has already been stated in regard to the Sacrament of Penance applies with greater force to this Sacrament. The only question is in regard to the knowledge required.

(a). *Cases in which it is possible to instruct the subject.*—Much will depend on the circumstances, but if necessity urges, it will be sufficient to instruct the subject in a general way, if he has not sufficient information already, that the Sacrament is a spiritual remedy for the soul, and not a merely medical process or superstitious rite.

(b). *Cases in which instruction is impossible.*—If the infirm person, when in possession of his senses,

---

67 I. e., unless external reconciliation has taken place. In case the dying man is destitute of the senses, and no sign has been nor can be given, the Church does not judge the occult in the external forum, and so he is considered juridically as remaining externally in his previous condition. Cfr. Coll., no. 1116, concerning contumacious Masons, and S. C. S. Off., July 6, ad 3 et 4, Coll., no. 2007, which concerns a case in which conditional absolution is given to a dying non-Catholic, but the *cautiones* are demanded.

68 Canon 855, no. 1.

sought or seemingly sought Extreme Unction at least implicitly, even though he then lost his senses or the use of reason, nevertheless the Sacrament is to be administered absolutely.[69] If even this condition is not manifestly satisfied, the canon does not exclude the giving of conditional Extreme Unction. Theologians teach that it can be conferred conditionally, which is confirmed by the 1916 response.[70]

(c). *Persons who were formal heretics.*—Extreme Unction is not to be conferred on those who contumaciously persist impenitent in manifest mortal sin; but if there is doubt, it is to be conferred conditionally.[71] In case the dying man is destitute of his senses, and no sign has or can be given, there is no certainty regarding the endurance of contumacy.[72] The difference between this canon and the analogous one on Holy Communion is important; here contumacy, which demands knowledge of subjective conditions,[73] is in question, but in the case of the Holy Eucharist, it was the public state, without reference to the subjective conditions.[74] Hence, there can be no difficulty concerning the conditional administration of Extreme Unction to such a dying person, under the circumstances.[75] But some theologians oppose this conclusion.[76]

3. *Confirmation.*

The Code contains only one canon on Confirmation, which expressly concerns *infantes,* in danger of

69 Canon 943.

70 Vermeersch, *Theo. Mor.,* III, no. 202; Pesch, *Prae. Theo. Dogm.,* VII, no. 551. Cfr. chapter II, sec. 3.

71 Canon 942.

72 Vermeersch-Creusen, II, no. 226; Genicot, *Inst. Theo. Mor.,* II, no. 423; Blat, *Comm. Test. C. J. C., Lib.* III, *Pars* I, p. 339-340, seems to accept this view practically.

73 Cfr. this chapter, sec. 1, 5.

74 Cfr. canon 855, no. 1: ". . . publice indigni . . ."; and canon 942; ". . . contumaciter. . . ."

75 Cfr. chapter II, sec. 3.

76 Cfr. Pesch, op. c., VII, Noldin, *Theo. Mor.,* II, no. 444, c. (although in an extreme case).

death.[77] Pope Benedict XIV regulated that this Sacrament should not be conferred until the subject had some knowledge of its nature. The Congregation of the Council pointed out that the subject did not have to be so old as for First Communion. In the Eastern Church, and in some particular regions of the West, Confirmation is administered to infants. The Code contains these modifications as a general law so that Confirmation can be conferred on a dying *infans* before the age of seven.

In the case of adults, past responses required some knowledge of the nature of the Sacrament, even in the case of the dying. But it is not required for the valid reception of the Sacrament, as the Code states that anyone be confirmed licitly and fruitfully, he must be in the state of grace and if he enjoys the use of reason, sufficiently instructed.[78]

No obligation of administering the Sacrament under such circumstances is imposed: although this Sacrament is not necessary by necessity of means for salvation, it is lawful for no one, *data occasione,* to neglect it; finally, *parochi* should take care that the faithful approach it at an opportune time.[79]

Hence, if the dying person is a baptized neophyte, or has been formally converted on his deathbed, it is seemingly unreasonable to refuse Confirmation, if it can be conferred and scandal avoided. Prudence will be the determining factor, if one has the necessary faculties. If there is danger of greater evils, is can be omitted.

77 Canon 788.
78 Canon 786.
79 Canon 787.

CHAPTER VI.

DYING NON-CATHOLICS AND THE SACRAMENT OF MATRIMONY.

No difficulty will be present in cases where the dying man formally converts to the Catholic faith. He is then regarded as a Catholic, and no impediment exists from viewpoint of mixed religion or disparity of worship. Hence, in this chapter only cases of doubtful conversion or those in which the dying man is unconverted are considered. Throughout the discussion the dying party is always the non-Catholic, and the only impediment considered is that arising from the difference of religion of this party.

1. *Powers Granted to Ordinaries.*

"In danger of death, Ordinaries may, for the relief of conscience and, if the case demands it, for the legitimation of children, grant dispensation, both from the form of marriage, and from each and all of the ecclesiastical impediments, whether public or occult, even if there are several, excepting the impediment of priestly Orders and affinity in the direct life arising from consummatd marriage, to their subjects, wherever they may be, and to all persons actually in their territory, care being taken to avoid scandal, and if dispensation is granted from the impediment of disparity of cult or mixed religion, the usual guarantees being exacted."[1]

2. *Powers Granted to Priests.*

"Under the circumstances described in canon 1043, but only in those cases in which even the Ordinary of

1 Canon 1043. Cfr. Ayrinhac, *Marriage Legislation in the New Code of Canon Law*, p. 86-87.

the place could not be reached, the same power of dispensing is enjoyed by the pastor and by the priest who assists at a marriage in accordance with the provision of can. 1098, par. 2, and by the confessor; but this last one in the internal forum only and in the act of sacramental confession."[2]

3. *Extraordinary Circumstances.*

"If it is impossible without grave inconvenience to send for or go to a pastor or Ordinary or a priest delegated by either of these to assist at a marriage in accordance with the prescriptions of canons 1095, 1096:

"1. In case of danger of death, marriage will be contracted validly and licitly in presence of the witnesses only. . . .

"2. In both cases if a priest could be present he should assist at the marriage, together with the witnesses, but the marriage would be valid in the presence of the witnesses alone."[3]

4. *Analysis.*

As the dying person in the present thesis is a non-Catholic, and publicly known as such, it follows that the impediments in question will always be public. Hence, there is no need for a treatment of the power of the confessor in such cases.

(a). *The nature of the power granted.*—Before the Code the power of the Ordinary in these cases was delegated. In 1888, with the original faculty, the Ordinary was given the power of subdelegating one person,[4] which was extended in 1889 so that the Ordinary could habitually subdelegate also all *parochi*, but only *parochi*.[5] In a response on the Ne Temere, the priest in exceptional extraordinary cases was granted

2 Canon 1044. Cfr. Ayrinhac, op. c., p. 88-89.
3 Canon 1098. Cfr. Ayrinhac, op. c., p. 246.
4 Litt. encycl., S. C. S. Off., February 20, 1888, Coll., no. 1685.
5 S. C. S. Off., April 23, 1890, Coll., no. 1728.

the same power as the Ordinary, but thus delegated *a jure.*[6] By a further response of 1910, it was declared that this also included all *parochi,* so that they became delegated *a jure* also.[7] The Ordinary was limited to cases in which there was not time to recur to the Holy See, the *parochus* to those in which there was not time to recur to the Ordinary, and the priest acting in extraordinary circumstances, from the very nature of his position, to cases where neither the Ordinary nor the *parochus* nor the delegate of either could be present.

In the Code the power of the Ordinary, conceded by canon 1043, is certainly ordinary, as it is *a jure* and attached to an office.[8] There is no restrictive clause, as in the old faculties, so that it can be exercised, regardless of whether there is time to recur to the Holy See or not. The power of the *parochus* is certainly ordinary for the internal forum, and according to some probably also ordinary for the external forum.[9] In the law in vogue before the Code, the supporters of the opposite view maintain that the *parochus* had no jurisdiction in the external forum. But, they say, the Code is altogether silent on the matter, so that the old law must be followed, according to canon 6, par. 4.[10] The question, however, is purely speculative, and the fact remains that the *parochus* can dispense from all contained in canon 1043, under precisely the same conditions and limitations provided therein, and habitually delegate others to do the same. The *parochus* is limited by the Code to cases "in quibus ne loci quidem Ordinarius adiri possit," without the added condition of the old faculty, "et periculum sit in mora." The

6 *Ne Temere* VII; May 14, 1909, AAS, I, p. 468.

7 July 29, 1910, AAS, II, p. 656.

8 Cfr. canons 145, no. 1, and 197, no. 2.

9 Vermeersch-Creusen, II, no. 353; Cappello, *De Sacramentis,* III, no. 236. *Contra,* Vlaming, *Prac. J. Mat.,* II, no. 415.

10 Vlaming, l. c.

power of the priest present under extraordinary circumstances is delegated *a jure* for both *fora,* as he has not an office in the strict sense.[11] He is limited to cases in which it is impossible without grave inconvenience to send for or go to a pastor or Ordinary or a priest delegated by either of these to assist at a marriage in accordance with the prescriptions of canons 1095, 1096. It is understood that the Ordinary and pastor in question are those who *a jure* validly assist at all marriages within their territory, i.e., the pastor of the place in which the party is dying. If the non-Catholic party is baptized, the marriage could be contracted validly, even without the *cautiones,* although illicitly, in the presence of two witnesses, and even though the priest in question be present. This conclusion flows logically from the fact that mixed religion, as distinguished from disparity of worship, is not a diriment impediment, and canon 1098, par. 2, expressly states "a marriage would be valid in the presence of two witnesses alone." The presence of the priest is necessary to grant the dispensation, but not for the validity of the marriage, not otherwise invalidated by some diriment impediment.

(b). *The persons over whom the power can be exercised.*—It is clear that this faculty can be exercised over subjects in one's own territory.[12] This was exceptional wherever the *Tametsi* bound, as it required the *Ordinarius proprius* or the *parochus proprius.* The *Ne Temere* changed the law regarding the *parochus proprius,* making it possible for a *parochus* to marry validly all, not otherwise subject to a diriment impediment, within his own territory, whether they were his subjects or not. The *Ne Temere* required three conditions that a marriage be

11 Vermeersch-Creusen, II, no. 353, 2.

12 Motry, *Diocesan Faculties,* p. 132-133, Washington, 1922.

celebrated without the competent priest: first, imminent *periculum mortis;* secondly, that the marriage be necessary "ad consulendum conscientiae et (si casus ferat) legitimationi prolis"; and, thirdly, that some priest be present.[13] The Code has modified the general canon 1098, so that *periculum* not *articulus mortis* suffices, no *necessitas conscientiae* is necessary, and the presence of the priest is not required *per se* for validity. Canons 1043 and 1044, however, contain the first two conditions, and if a diriment impediment be present the presence of the priest will be necessary to grant the dispensation. The Code follows the *Ne Temere,* but adds to this by allowing the Ordinary or *parochus* to exercise this faculty anywhere over his own subjects. The power of the priest acting according to canon 1098, par. 2, is obviously exercised over parties that are not his subjects.

(c). *The extent of the faculty.*—The original faculty did not include prohibitive or expressly occult impediments. A question was asked on April 23, 1890, as to whether the Ordinaries could habitually delegate the power of dispensing in such cases from occult impediments which they had in cases of most urgent necessity, according to the common opinion of theologians. The response was: "Ex vi decreti, affirmative pro mortis articulo."[14] The *Ne Temere* used general terms, but not until 1916 was it certain that the ecclesiastical form could be dispensed from, permitting the absence of the priest, but requiring the presence of two witnesses to the act itself of renewing the consent.[15] The Code is most generous and extends expressly the faculty so as to include the form, and all

13 Vermeersch-Creusen, II, no. 404.

14 S. C. S. Off., April 23, 1890, Coll., no. 1728.

15 S. C. S. Off., December 13, 1899, Coll., no. 2072; S. C. S. Off., August 2, 1916, AAS, VIII, p. 316.

ecclesiastical impediments, with the usual two exceptions, public or occult, diriment or prohibitive, single or multiple. The pastor enjoys the same faculty, and also the priest assisting at the marriage under extraordinary circumstances. Canon 1043 grants to Ordinaries the power of dispensing from the canonical form and certain impediments. Canon 1044 grants to *parochi* and the priest in the extraordinary case *eadem dispensandi facultate,* but canon 1043 stated: ". . . Ordinarii . . . possunt tum super forma . . . tum super omnibus et singulis impedimentis . . . dispensare. . . ." In any case in virtue of canon 1098, par. 2, although the priest's presence would be necessary for the granting of the dispensation from the impediment, it is not for the validity of the marriage, *salva conjugii validitate coram solis testibus.* This opinion is confirmed by the previous decision of 1919, which affords an example of a justifying cause.[16] The same reason may exist for granting the dispensation from the form in the case of the pastor as the Ordinary, e.g., difficulties from the civil law in emergency cases, where the parties are married before securing the necessary marriage license. Moreover, the powers conceded in canons 1043 and 1044 are subject to broad interpretation.[17]

(d). *Requirements on the part of the subject.*—In the original grant the parties had to be either previously civilly married or living in concubinage. The *Ne Temere* did not contain these restrictions, and used words similar to the Code, which place absolutely no such restrictions as to whether the marriage is to be contracted, or was contracted invalidly in the past, or

16 S. C. de Sacrs., May 14, 1919, AAS, VIII, p. 36: in periculo mortis . . . "quilibet sacerdos dispensare valet etiam ab impedimento clandestinitatis, permittendo ut in relatis adjunctis matrimonium cum solis testibus valide et licite contrahatur."

17 Cfr. canons 199, no. 1, 200, no. 1, 202.

was merely concubinage without even the appearance of marriage, etc.

The Code gives two conditions under which the faculty can be used, as all canonists agree that the *et* is disjunctive, which the clause *si casus ferat* placed before the second alternative renders certain. It was already clear before the Code that the faculty could be used where the impediment mainly affected the party in good health.[18] Hence, there must be one of two conditions present, either the relief of conscience, or the legitimation of the offspring, in cases such as this thesis considers.[18b]

(e). *Removal of scandal.*—The most effective means of removing scandal, with certain exceptions, is the making known of the marriage. This may not be possible, either because it involves great danger, or gives rise to a greater scandal. Thus, if a marriage license has not been obtained, heavy civil penalties may be incurred. If it is possible to obtain such, and the marriage takes place after it is obtained, ordinarily publication of the marriage will remove scandal. But if the license has not been obtained, its publication would be rash. In cases in which ordained clerics, of the rank of subdeacon or deacon, or persons with solemn vows, the Holy See in the past has recommended secrecy in the matter of the marriage, and removal to other parts where the facts are unknown, as the

18 S. C. S. Off., July 1, 1891, Coll., no. 1758. Cfr. S. C. S. Off., July 6, 1898, ad 3 et 4, Coll., no. 2007, which declared that the faculty could be used in the case of an infidel civilly married to a Catholic, who is *sui compos and dying*, provided the matrimonial consent was renewed and the *cautiones* given If there was a possible hope of the future Catholic instruction of the children, they were to be baptized; if not, only in case they were *in articulo mortis*. In such a case, the *cautiones* are to be demanded from the Catholic party, if he is still *sui compos*.

18b Vlaming no. 401, p. 24; Genicot, II, no. 522: "In Codice legitur *et*, si cut in decr. *Ne temere* ubi de facultate assistendi matromonio in extremis. Sed consentiebant commentatores alterutram causam sufficere." Vermeersch-Creusen, II, no. 348; Cappello, III, no. 232, d.

method of avoiding scandal.[19]

(f). *The Cautiones.*—The Holy See in the past demanded that the *cautiones* should be sought, even *in articulo mortis.*[20] Before the Code, the general faculty was in all cases delegated, and did not cover mixed marriage, as distinguished from disparity of worship. In certain regions, e.g., parts of Germany, Hungary, Austria, and Chile, the passive assistance of the priest was tolerated at marriages, which remained illicit, due to the absence of the *cautiones,* because of the civil law. Thus, by a Letter of the Cardinal Secretary of State, March 27, 1830, faculties were granted by which the bishops could not dispense, but "idcirco tantum eo in casu relaxari ne graviora scandala eveniant," and with the exclusion of all ecclesiastical rite of any kind.[20b] This was repeated by an Apostolic Letter of Gregory XVI, April 30, 1841.[21] In an Instruction of the Propaganda Fidei, 1858, addressed to the Greco-Rumenian bishops, a similar toleration was granted.[22] In the last two cases the expression *quamvis illicita, provalidis habenda* is used. In a response of the Holy Office, July 6, 1898, concerning a case in which the Catholic party had been civilly married, and had children by a Jew, in which it would seem that the *cautiones* could not be secured from the non-Catholic party: "A moribundo catholico vero, si iam est compos sui, cautiones exquirantur ut praedicta valeant obtineri."[23] The Holy Office, April 12, 1899, declared that in cases in which the *cautiones* could not be secured, the Pope should be asked for a *sanatio in radice*

19 Litt. encycl. S. C. S. Off., February 20, 1888, Coll., no. 1685, *Mens.* Cfr. De Smet, *Betrothment and Marriage,* I, no. 135.

20 S. C. S. Off., March 18, 1891, Coll., no. 1750.

20b Footnote added to Litt. Ap. Pii PP. VIII, March 25, 1830, Coll., no. 811 (Coll., vol. I, p. 476).

21 Litt. Ap. Gregorii PP. XVI, April 30, 1841, Coll., no. 920.

22 Instr. S. C. de Prop. F., 1858, Coll., no. 1154 (*versus finem*).

23 S. C. S. Off., July 6, 1898, Coll., no. 2007.

with the perseverance of consent.[24] On June 21, 1912, a general decree was issued which stated: "In concedendis ab habente S. Sede potestatem dispensationibus super impedimento disparitatis cultus praescriptae cautiones semper sunt exigendae et si vero his cautionibus non requisitis vel denegatis dispensatio detur, pro nulla habenda est, et matrimonium ex hoc capite esse nullum per se ipsum Ordinarius declarare potest, *quin singulis vicibus ad S. Sedem pro definitiva sententia recurrat.*"[25] Whatever about the decision of 1912, it can be stated that previous to 1912 there was a real *dubium legis,* so that documents previous to that date will not establish certainty with regard to the Code.

Canons 1043 and 1044 grant powers which are ordinary, and so essentially change the whole question. The responses and decrees of the old law in reference to this faculty, then, concern delegated and not ordinary jurisdiction. Hence, the canons in question have to be taken on their own merits. But canon 1043, in reference to the *cautiones* contains an ablative absolute clause *praestitis consuetis cautionibus,* which does not necessarily involve a condition that is required absolutely for validity.[26] Before the Code, in the case of a general law, the force of such a clause was vigorously disputed. The common opinion was that it did not pertain to validity, unless this was demanded by the very nature of things. Hence, a *dubium juris* would exist before the Code in regard to the irritating force of such a clause in a general law. But after the Code, there is hardly room for doubt, as canon 15 expressly states: "Leges, etiam irritantes et inhabilitantes, in dubio juris non urgent . . . ," and

---

24 S. C. S. Off., April 12, 1899, Coll., no. 2042.

25 Ad 1, AAS, IV, p. 442.

26 Cfr. Vermeersch-Creusen, I, no. 114, citing D'Annibale, I, 76; III, 500 et 502.

canon 11: "Irritantes aut inhabilitantes eae tantum leges habendae sunt, quibus aut actum esse nullum aut inhabilem esse personam expresse vel aequivalenter statuitur." But it is not clear from the ablative absolute clause used in the present instance that the exercise of the power of dispensing, in the absence of the *cautiones,* is null. In the very same canon (1043) another ablative absolute clause is used, *remoto scandalo,* which all agree does not pertain to the validity of the faculty. An argument from analogy might be drawn from the canons regarding rescripts, and the force of the clauses contained in them. Before the Code, the same dispute about the ablative absolute clause prevailed, but canon 39 states some of the particles required for validity, but does not expressly include the disputed ablative absolute. Hence, some canonists have concluded that the silence is positive, and it does not pertain to validity, unless this is clear from the nature of things.[26b] Incidentally, the same clause refers to both mixed religion, which is only a prohibiting impediment, and disparity of cult.

It is clear from the nature of things that neither the impediments of mixed religion nor disparity of worship derive their complete force from the divine law. Mixed religion is only a prohibitive impediment in the ecclesiastical law,[27] and as we are considering the irritating force of the impediments, no further discussion is necessary. The very definition of disparity of worship as found in the Code proves beyond dispute that the irritating force is ecclesiastical.[28] Thus, it only exists between a person baptized in the Catholic

26b Vermeersch-Creusen, I, no. 114; Marota, no. 284; ". . . ablativo absoluto, etc., continent dumtaxat id quod jam ex ipsa natura rei, de qua agitur aut ex iure esset praestandum . . ." Both cite D'Annibale.

27 Canon 1060.

28 Canon 1070.

Church, or converted from heresy or schism to it, and an unbaptized person, as a diriment impediment.

But are the *cautiones* demanded for the valid exercise of the ordinary power of dispensing? It is quite clear that if the Church by positive law gave the dirimenting force to the impediment, it can dispense validly to this extent at least in all cases. Thus, the Code itself has relaxed the dirimenting force for all those baptized persons, leaving the divine law untouched, who do not fall under the definition of disparity of worship. In the past, the power of relaxing the law, leaving the illiceity untouched, was tolerated by the Church, at least as far as the impediment of mixed religion is concerned. It was never denied that the Pope, who exercises supreme ordinary power, could validly dispense or relax the force of the ecclesiastical law. But the nature of the power of inferiors in 1043 and 1044 has been changed by the Code itself from delegated to ordinary, which withdraws all the restrictions of the past, and permits of its interpretation according to the law of the Code alone. The fact that in the past the Holy See in specific instances and requests for faculties to dispense where the *cautiones* could not be secured preferred to grant the delegated power of *sanatio in radice* does not materially affect the question. A *sanatio* from its definition implicitly contains a dispensation, heals the marriage from its inception, and operates where the renewal of consent is impossible.[29] If the party is willing to renew his consent in some form for convalidation of an attempted marriage, or is willing to give it for the first time in a marriage to be contracted, a *sanatio* will not be necessary in the first case, and impossible in the second.

29 Canon 1138, no. 1: "Matrimonii in radice sanatio est eiusdem convalidatio, secumferens, praeter dispensationem vel cessationem impedimenti, dispensationem a lege de renovando consensu, et retrotractionem, per fictionem iuris, circa effectus canonicos, ad praeteritum."

But will this be possible without obtaining the *cautiones,* or where they have been refused? In other words, if the faculty is used in such cases, will the marriage be invalid? In the case of mixed marriages, where both parties are baptized, as the impediment itself has not dirimenting force, it is clear that the marriage is valid. But where the non-Catholic party is unbaptized? There is no expressly irritating clause contained in canon 1043, so that the general law will have to be inspected.

The faculties granted in canons 1043 and 1044 are *ipso jure,* so that they must be exercised under the general law of the Code itself. Canon 1061, concerning the *cautiones,* reads somewhat as follows:

> "No. 1. The Church grants no dispensation from the impediment of mixed religion, unless:
>
> "1. There be just and grave causes;
>
> "2. The non-Catholic party give guarantees that the danger of perversion for the Catholic party will be removed, and both parties promise that all the children will be baptized and brought up only in the Catholic faith.
>
> "3. There be a moral certainty that the promises be fulfilled.
>
> "No. 2. Regularly the promises should be demanded in writing."[30]

The same canon applies to disparity of cult.[31] The first condition in the first paragraph is certainly required for validity by reason of canon 84, par. 1, which governs the action of inferiors to the Pope. The ecclesiastical law must not be dispensed unless there is a just and reasonable cause, proportionate to the gravity of the law dispensed from; otherwise a dis-

30 Canon 1061. Cfr. Ayrinhac, p. c., p. 117.
31 Canon 1071.

pensation granted by an inferior is illicit and invalid. The second condition presents the real difficulty. Even *in articulo mortis,* past decrees of the Holy See have insisted that the *cautiones* should be demanded.

The divine law demands that the Catholic party shall not place himself in the proximate danger of perversion, and the same applies to the children of such a marriage. It demands for the liceity, not the validity, of marriages with persons or non-Catholics that these conditions be either absent in the case or rendered remote. The probable danger of death of the non-Catholic may remove the immediate occasion of perversion for the Catholic party, as far as the divine law is concerned. Thus, the danger of death, and moral certainty of actual death before the use of reason, is considered as sufficient removal of the danger of perversion, in the case of infants of infidels.[32] But in the absence of the *cautiones,* there is danger in the case of the children in the future, either due to the recovery of non-Catholic party, or the enactments of civil law. Hence, if the *cautiones* are not obtained, which are a concrete determination of the conditions of the divine law, the marriage will be illicit. Under these circumstances, the Church, through the Pope, and those to whom he has conceded the power, can dispense validly and licitly from the dirimenting force of the impediment of disparity of worship, leaving the obligation of the divine law untouched. But in such cases, past decrees clearly show that the Church does not wish her ministers to take any active part. Under canons 1043 and 1044, it will not be necessary for the minister to assist passively, as he also has power to dispense from the canonical form, and render the marriage valid, if entered into before witnesses.

32 Canon 750, no. 1.

Canon 1061, par. 1, no. 2, certainly contains no irritating clause. The general introductory clause of the paragraph does not supply this defect, as it covers also the third condition of the same paragraph, which all concede does not pertain to the validity of the dispensation. But the canon itself must contain this clause, either expressly or equivalently.[33] Moreover, in the delegated faculties granted, usually a certainly invalidating clause introduced by the particle *dummodo* is used.[34] In the wartime faculties, however, granted by the Consistorial Congregation, April 25, 1918, this was not contained, but . . . "Ordinarius prae oculis semper habeat regulas statutas in Codice lib. III, tit. VII, cap. 2, 3, et 4, circa impedimenta in genere et in specie itemque clausulas apponi solitas in matrimoniis cum hebraeis et mahumetanis . . ."[35] Thus, it calls special attention to two types of marriages with the impediment of worship, but leaves the others to the regulations in the Code.

Commentators, writing after the Code, are not at all agreed on the force of the ablative absolute clause regarding the *cautiones* in canon 1043.[36] One of great weight has changed his view, and declared that the opinion which permits the valid use of the faculty in 1043 without them as *probabilior.*[37] Some prefer to apply canon 81: Ordinaries inferior of the Roman

33 Canon 11.

34 E. g., Baltimore.

35 Cfr. Cappello, *De Sacramentis,* III, p. 258 (footnote).

36 The cautiones are not for validity in canon 1043, Vermeersch, *Theo. Mor.,* III, no. 758 (1923), who cites Pighi and Cerato in favor of this view; Genicot, *Inst. Theo. Mor.,* II, no. 522; Cappello, *De Sacrs.,* III, no. 232; Petrovits, *The New Church Law on Matrimony,* nos. 160, 189. De Smet, op. c., says the cautiones are for the validity of canons 1043 and 1044, p. 103, note 4, but applies canon 81, by which Ordinary can grant valid dispensation without them in such cases, no. 508, p. 36, note 1, no. 512.

37 Vermeersch-Creusen, *Ep. J. C.,* II, no. 348, formerly held the negative opinion in year 1922, but grants that the other opinion is *probabilior* for canon 1043 and 1044 in his *Moral Theology,* III, no. 758, in year 1923.

Pontiff cannot dispense from the general laws of the Church, not even in a particular case, unless this power has been conceded to them explicitly or implicitly, or unless the *recursus* to the Holy See is difficult and at the same time there is danger of grave danger in the delay, and there is question of a dispensation which the Holy See is accustomed to grant.[38] In the case, however, either the conditions of the divine law are satisfied or they are not. If the former is the case, as there is no certainly irritating clause in either canon 1061 or 1043, the faculty is to receive a broad interpretation and the act of dispensing will be valid.[39] If the latter is true in the case, no one can licitly dispense from the divine law, but with sufficient reason, the faculty will be validly exercised, and marriage valid but illicit. But the Church has tolerated illicit marriages in the past. The *cautiones* will then be obtained from the Catholic party, but the minister will dispense from the canonical form also, and warn the Catholic party. If it is a case of a marriage already attempted, the faculty includes convalidation, but not *sanatio,* so that nothing can be done in the absence of special additional faculties, unless the parties are willing to renew the consent in some form. There is no longer need of special indults, which permit passive assistance in such cases, so that the Holy Office, November 26, 1919, responded in a general manner: "Contrariae S. Sedis praescriptiones atque contraria indulta per ipsum Codicem iuris canonici abrogata sunt."[40]

In the case, if the non-Catholic refuses to give the *cautiones,* which past responses declared were to be *exigendae* even *in articulo mortis,* obviously as he is

38 Canon 81, cfr. De Smet, op. c., II, p. 40 (footnote).
39 Canon 200, no. 1; cfr. canons 199, no. 1, 202.
40 Cited by Prümmer, *Manuale J. C.,* p. 413 (footnote), from *Linzer Quartalschrift,* 1921, 249.

the dying person in this thesis, offspring will have to exist. The fact of his dying condition, and the continued existence of the Catholic party is a guarantee of the absence of perversion of the Catholic. The Church would in any case baptize the children in such circumstances. Actually the divine law may be *de facto* better fulfilled in the case than by the obtaining of the *cautiones*, the giving of which and not the fulfilment is required by canon 1061. But in all cases, the *cautiones* must be secured for liceity. If there are no offspring, it is hard to see how there could be a just and sufficient cause to exercise the faculty with the denial of the *cautiones* as the *urgente mortis periculo* removes danger of concubinage, etc., for the present.

CONCLUSION.

The conclusion to this study can indeed be brief. After all, the last moments of every dying man are filled with mystery and the workings of Divine Providence.

Undoubtedly, the most unsatisfactory results have been those concerned with the possibility of baptizing those who gave and can give no signs. But is not the entire matter more or less one of the secrets, which, if the dying man does not recover, remains forever hidden? With great consolation, then, the writer cites a passage on the attitude of St. Augustine on certain kindred problems:

> As for the second case of simulation which concerns Baptism conferred with the obvious end of amusement or mockery, St. Augustine refused to commit himself on the subject. Were he obliged to give an opinion on the value of such a Baptism, he would have recourse to prayer, and would await the true solution from Divine revelation.[1] "Divinum judicium per alicujus revelationis oraculum, concordi oratione et impensis supplici devotione gemitibus implorandum esse censerem." The Bishop of Hippo was convinced that God communicates Divine truth by a sort of direct revelation, whenever the doctors of the Church need it and ask it in fervent prayer. It was by a revelation of this kind that he was taught when he wrote towards the year 397 to Simplicianus, Bishop of Milan, that the beginning of faith is a gift of grace; up till then he thought otherwise.[2] And did not St. Thomas Aquinas himself declare that he learned directly from God through prayer much more than by all his studies"?[3]

3 Pourrat, *Theology of the Sacraments,* p. 368-369, who cites (1) *Epist.* clxxiii, no. 103, and (2) *De praedestin,* no. 8.

Lest, then, in searching too eagerly the mysteries of Divine Providence, as the Apostles sought to know the time of the Last Day, one finds the indications of the destruction of Jerusalem intertwined, the final solution of this difficult problem is left where it always was—a mystery of Divine Providence.

DEUS LUX MEA

THESES

QUAS

AD DOCTORATUS GRADUM

IN

Iure Canonico

APUD UNIVERSITATEM
CATHOLICAM AMERICAE

CONSEQUENDUM

PUBLICE PROPUGNABIT

IACOBUS IGNATIUS KING

SACERDOS ARCHIDIOECESIS SANCTI PAULI

JURIS CANONICI LICENTIATUS

HORA XI A. M. DIE XXVII MAII A. D. MCMXXIV.

Universitas Catholica Americæ

Washingtonii, D. C.

Facultas Juris Canonici

1923-1924

No. 23.

I. Sources of International Law.
II. Recognition of a State.
III. General Rights and Obligations of States.
IV. Protectorates, Suzerainties, Spheres of Influence, Mandates.
V. Immunities and Privileges of Diplomatic Agents.
VI. Piracy.
VII. Jurisdiction over Vessels.
VIII. The Monroe Doctrine.
IX. Extradition.
X. Consuls.
XI. De Erroribus quoad Formam Regiminis Ecclesiae.
XII. De Cessatione Protestatis Romani Pontificis.
XIII. De Jure Gladii.
XIV. De Potestate Magisteriali.
XV. An Potestas Jurisdictionis episcopalis sit immediate a deo?
XVI. De Natura et Limitibus Jurisdictionis episcopalis.
XVII. De Ratione et Natura Parochiatus.
XVIII. De Jure Civili quoad Matrimonium.
XIX. De Relatione Ecclesiae ad Principium Libertatis religiosae.
XX. De Concordatis in genere.
XXI. Canones 5-7.
XXII. Canones 12-14.
XXIII. Canones 36-37.
XXIV. Canones 80-86.

XXV. Canones 90-95.
XXVI. Canones 196-209.
XXVII. Canones 518-530.
XXVIII. Canones 637-645.
XXIX. Canon 731.
XXX. Canones 749-751.
XXXI. Canones 752, 754.
XXXII. Canones 882.
XXXIII. Canones 892-900.
XXXIV. Canones 940-944.
XXXV. Canones 1043-1044.
XXXVI. Canones 1060-1064.
XXXVII. Canones 1239-1242.
XXXVIII. Canones 1243-1246.
XXXIX. Canones 1307-1315.
XL. Canones 1372-1383.
XLI. Canones 1556-1568.
XLII. Canones 1560.
XLIII. Canones 1561-1566.
XLIV. Canones 1586-1590.
XLV. Canones 1648-1651.
XLVI. Canone 1654.
XLVII. Canones 1679-1883.
XLVIII. Canones 1690-1692.
XLIX. Canones 1701-1705.
L. Canones 1742-1746.
LI. Canones 1756-1758.
LII. Canones 2241-2242.
LIII. Canones 2252-2254.
LIV. Canones 2286-2289.
LV. Canones 2312-2313.
LVI. Canon 2314.
LVII. Canon 2319.

LVIII. Canon 2335.
LIX. Canon 2350.
LX. Canon 2375.

Vidit Sacra Facultas:

PHILLIPPUS BERNARDINI, J.U.D., S.T.D., Decanus.

HUBERTUS LUDOVICUS MOTRY, J.C.D., S.T.D., a Secretis.

Vidit Rector Universitatis:

✠ THOMAS J. SHAHAN, S.T.D., J.U.L.

BIOGRAPHY.

James Ignatius King was born May 13, 1895, in Belfast, Ireland. He received his college course under the Jesuit Fathers at St. Michael's College, Leeds, Yorkshire, England, and seminary course at The St. Paul Seminary, St. Paul, Minnesota, where he was ordained priest by the Rt. Rev. Austin Dowling, 1922. In 1922 he entered The Catholic University of America, Washington, D. C., and pursued theological studies under the direction of Monsignor Dr. Phillipp Bernardini, Dr. John A. Ryan, Dr. Hubert L. Motry, Dr. Valentine T. Schaaf, and Dr. Fitzgerald, to all of whom he hereby expresses his sincere thanks.

www.ingramcontent.com/pod-product-compliance
Lightning Source LLC
LaVergne TN
LVHW050214080826
844660LV00012B/411

* 9 7 8 0 8 1 3 2 2 2 1 4 1 *